Male Olympic Champions

Other Books in the History Makers Series:

Male Olympic Champions

By Michael V. Uschan

Lucent Books
P.O. Box 289011, San Diego, CA 92198-9011

For Ryan Shimabakuro, a speed skater from Hawaii, and every other athlete who has never won a medal or even had a chance to compete in the Olympics, but whose pursuit of excellence has embodied the Olympic spirit defined by Baron Pierre de Coubertin:

The most important thing in the Olympic Games is not to win but to take part, just as the most important thing in life is not the triumph but the struggle. The essential thing is not to have conquered but to have fought well.

Library of Congress Cataloging-in-Publication Data

Uschan, Michael V., 1948–
    Male Olympic champions / by Michael V. Uschan.
      p.   cm. — (History makers)
    Includes bibliographical references (p.) and index.
    Summary: A discussion of the spirit and evolution of the Olympic games preceeds accounts of seven Olympic champions: Jim Thorpe, Paavo Nurmi, Jesse Owens, Jean-Claude Killy, Mark Spitz, Vasily Alexeyev, and Eric Heiden.
    ISBN 1-56006-614-8 (lib. : alk. paper)
    1. Athletes—Bibliography—Juvenile literature.   2. Olympics—Juvenile literature. [1. Athletes. 2. Olympics.] I. Title. II. Series.
  GV697.AIU83 2000
  796'.081'0922—dc21

                                 99-040332

                                  CIP
                                  AC

Printed in the U.S.A.

Contents

FOREWORD

The literary form most often referred to as "multiple biography" was perfected in the first century A.D. by Plutarch, a perceptive and talented moralist and historian who hailed from the small town of Chaeronea in central Greece. His most famous work, *Parallel Lives*, consists of a long series of biographies of noteworthy ancient Greek and Roman statesmen and military leaders. Frequently, Plutarch compares a famous Greek to a famous Roman, pointing out similarities in personality and achievements. These expertly constructed and very readable tracts provided later historians and others, including playwrights like Shakespeare, with priceless information about prominent ancient personages and also inspired new generations of writers to tackle the multiple biography genre.

The Lucent History Makers series proudly carries on the venerable tradition handed down from Plutarch. Each volume in the series consists of a set of five to eight biographies of important and influential historical figures who were linked together by a common factor. In *Rulers of Ancient Rome*, for example, all the figures were generals, consuls, or emperors of either the Roman Republic or Empire; while the subjects of *Fighters Against American Slavery*, though they lived in different places and times, all shared the same goal, namely the eradication of human servitude. Mindful that politicians and military leaders are not (and never have been) the only people who shape the course of history, the editors of the series have also included representatives from a wide range of endeavors, including scientists, artists, writers, philosophers, religious leaders, and sports figures.

Each book is intended to give a range of figures—some well known, others less known; some who made a great impact on history, others who made only a small impact. For instance, by making Columbus's initial voyage possible, Spain's Queen Isabella I, featured in *Women Leaders of Nations*, helped to open up the New World to exploration and exploitation by the European powers. Unarguably, therefore, she made a major contribution to a series of events that had momentous consequences for the entire world. By contrast, Catherine II, the eighteenth-century Russian queen, and Golda Meir, the modern Israeli prime minister, did not play roles of global impact; however, their policies and actions significantly influenced the historical development of both their own countries and their regional neighbors. Regardless of their relative importance in the greater historical scheme, all of the figures chronicled in the History Makers series made contributions to posterity; and their public achievements, as well as what is known about their private lives, are presented and evaluated in light of the most recent scholarship.

In addition, each volume in the series is documented and substantiated by a wide array of primary and secondary source quotations. The primary source quotes enliven the text by presenting eyewitness views of the times and culture in which each history maker lived; while the secondary source quotes, taken from the works of respected modern scholars, offer expert elaboration and/ or critical commentary. Each quote is footnoted, demonstrating to the reader exactly where biographers find their information. The footnotes also provide the reader with the means of conducting additional research. Finally, to further guide and illuminate readers, each volume in the series features photographs, two bibliographies, and a comprehensive index.

The History Makers series provides both students engaged in research and more casual readers with informative, enlightening, and entertaining overviews of individuals from a variety of circumstances, professions, and backgrounds. No doubt all of them, whether loved or hated, benevolent or cruel, constructive or destructive, will remain endlessly fascinating to each new generation seeking to identify the forces that shaped their world.

The Olympic Champion: Swifter, Higher, Stronger

Baron Pierre de Coubertin, the French sports enthusiast who in 1896 resurrected the Olympic Games in their historic homeland of Greece, never believed it mattered which athlete won an event or which country collected the most medals. Claimed de Coubertin:

> The most important thing in the Olympic Games is not to win but to take part, just as the most important thing in life is not the triumph but the struggle. The essential thing is not to have conquered but to have fought well.[1]

True to the spirit of de Coubertin's words, fans of the Olympics have always had a soft spot in their hearts for the athlete who tries valiantly, only to fail. In 1908 diminutive Dorando Pietri, a candy maker from Italy, was the first to enter White City Stadium in London, England, at the conclusion of the marathon. Overcome by the heat of the day and by exertion, Pietri collapsed several times as he bravely staggered the final few yards to victory. Spurred by appeals from concerned spectators, officials helped the dazed runner across the finish line; Pietri was then carried away on a stretcher and hospitalized.

When Johnny Hayes of the United States finished under his own power thirty-two seconds later, the U.S. team argued that officials should not have helped Pietri, and the Italian runner was disqualified. Hayes won the gold medal, but Pietri gained something nearly as important—the respect of the world for trying his best.

In the 1988 Winter Olympics, ski jumper Michael Edwards of Great Britain, nicknamed "Eddie the Eagle" by an admiring press corps, won the hearts of fans with his clumsy, gutsy attempt to compete against far superior jumpers. Little more than a novice at the dangerous sport, Edwards, a plasterer by trade who had to borrow skis from the Austrian team, admitted, "The most important thing for me was to survive."[2] Edwards was considered a "winner" because he was brave enough to jump so his country would be represented.

Officials help a dazed Dorando Pietri across the finish line of the 1908 Olympic marathon.

Yet the motivating spirit for athletes is more truly summed up in the Latin phrase adopted as the Olympic motto at the 1924 Summer Games in Paris, France: "Citius, Altius, Fortius." Translated as "Swifter, Higher, Stronger," the philosophy was first voiced by Henri Didon, a French Dominican monk who believed his students needed to develop their bodies as well as their minds.

Through the decades it has, indeed, been the athlete who runs faster, jumps higher, and is stronger who has captured the world's attention by winning a gold medal, the most treasured prize in amateur sports. This book details the lives of seven of the greatest Olympic champions, athletes whose abilities overwhelmed their competitors and amazed the world.

The Magnificent Seven

The first great Olympic champion was Native American Jim Thorpe, who won gold medals in the pentathlon and decathlon in 1912 and was hailed by King Gustav V of Sweden as the "greatest athlete in the world." Yet Thorpe's Olympic dream turned into a nightmare when officials stripped him of his medals after learning that he had played baseball professionally. Thorpe had received as little as $2 a game in a brief youthful foray into pro sports, but officials revoked his amateur status the year after the Olympics and took back his medals.

In 1920 Finland's Paavo Nurmi began earning his reputation as the greatest runner of all time by winning his first gold medal. He won nine gold medals in three Olympics through 1928, including a record five in 1924 in Paris, France. In 1924 Nurmi won the 1,500-meter race just a half-hour after taking gold in the 5,000-meter race; sportswriters called him a "superman" for his remarkable endurance.

In 1936 Jesse Owens, an African American whose grandparents had been slaves, destroyed Adolf Hitler's theory of Aryan supremacy by winning four events at the Olympics in Berlin, Germany. Hitler, who three years later would lead his nation in World War II, sat in grim silence each time Owens collected a medal.

When the 1968 Olympics came to Grenoble, France, native son Jean-Claude Killy swept the gold in the three Alpine skiing events—slalom, giant slalom, and downhill racing. One of the most daring, charismatic skiers of all time, Killy also headed the organization that returned the Winter Games to France in 1992.

Jim Thorpe was the first great Olympic champion, winning gold medals in the pentathlon and decathlon in the 1912 Games.

Jesse Owens (pictured with fellow runner Helen Stephens) destroyed Hitler's theory of Aryan supremacy by winning four events in the Berlin Olympics.

In 1972 American Mark Spitz won seven gold medals, dominating his sport as no swimmer ever had. However, his brilliant performance in Munich, Germany, was overshadowed by the worst tragedy in Olympic history, a terrorist attack that resulted in the deaths of eleven Israeli athletes.

For nearly a decade, Vasily Alexeyev was the world's strongest person. Competing for the Soviet Union, this huge, shaggy-haired bear of a man won gold medals in weight lifting in 1972 and 1976. Alexeyev was the first to lift 500 pounds, an awe-inspiring accomplishment that spurred comparisons with the mythical Hercules.

At the 1980 Olympics in Lake Placid, New York, Eric Heiden captured all five speed skating events, setting Olympic records at every distance from 500 to 10,000 meters. This U.S. skater's performance was all the more amazing because the sport had always been dominated by athletes from Europe, where speed skating is much more popular.

Olympic Gold

How great an achievement is it to win a gold medal? Roger Bannister of England will be remembered forever as the first to run the mile in less than 4 minutes (3:59.4), but even he realized his 1954 landmark race paled in comparison: "Records are ephemeral. The winning of an Olympic title is eternal."[3]

CHAPTER 1

Evolution of the Olympic Games

Spyridon Louis, a Greek who trained by running alongside his mule while transporting water from village to village, won the marathon to become the most famous champion of the first modern Olympics. A humble man, Louis after his victory rejected offers from grateful countrymen for free haircuts and free dinners for life. But when the king of Greece, George I, asked him if he had a special wish, Louis finally confessed his heart's desire: "Yes, please, a cart and a horse so I won't have to run after my mule any more."[4]

It was fitting that Louis won an event that, like the Olympics themselves, had its origins in his country's history. Fifty thousand spectators cheered madly April 10, 1896, when Louis crossed the finish line to end the race, which duplicated the twenty-five-mile route Greek courier Pheidippides ran to Athens in 490 B.C. from the battlefield of Marathon to announce a victory over the invading Persians.

But before Louis became a national hero and 311 athletes from thirteen countries would travel to Greece for a revived Olympics, a major organizational effort was required. That this effort was begun, and carried to completion, was due to the giant-sized dream of one small man—Baron Pierre de Coubertin.

The First Olympics

De Coubertin once said, "I was the sole author of the whole project."[5] It was no idle boast. Although the slight, short Frenchman (he was barely 5 feet, 3 inches tall) was dwarfed by participating athletes, the resurrection of the Olympics was sparked by his devotion to the high ideals he believed the Games represented. "The revival of the Olympic Games," de Coubertin claimed, "will bring athleticism to a high state of perfection and infuse a love for [peace] and a respect for life!"[6]

Born in Paris on January 1, 1863, to a family of wealth and aristocracy, de Coubertin believed sports could teach young people valuable lessons about honor, competition, and friendship. Profoundly affected as a young man by a visit to the original site of competition in Olympia, Greece, he resolved to resurrect the ancient Olympics. Held periodically since 776 B.C., the Games had been banned in A.D. 394 by a Roman emperor, Theodosius. The ruler, a Christian, considered the Games to be a pagan festival because they were dedicated to the mythical god Zeus. "Nothing in ancient history," de Coubertin wrote, "inspired more reverie in me than Olympia."[7]

Baron Pierre de Coubertin organized the first modern Olympics in 1896.

When de Coubertin invited representatives from a dozen countries to Paris in June 1894 to unveil his idea, the delegates eagerly embraced it, scheduling the first modern Olympics for 1896. The first Olympic champion in more than 1,500 years was James B. Connolly, a Harvard freshman who leaped 44 feet, 11 3/4 inches in the hop, step, and jump, an event known today as the triple jump. Connolly had to quit school to compete because Harvard refused him a leave of absence for what was then considered a minor sporting event.

The ancient Greek competition had been held every four years, a period called an Olympiad; the 1896 games were called Olympiad I and the second was held in 1900. The second and third Olympics were not very successful because they became mere sideshows for world fairs held in Paris, France, and St. Louis, Missouri.

The Olympics began to gain worldwide acceptance and recognition in 1908 in London, England, and four years later in Stockholm, Sweden, when Jim Thorpe won the pentathlon and decathlon. Already famous in his own country, the Sac and Fox Native American became the first Olympic champion revered internationally. And it is the star quality of gold medalists such as Thorpe that has made the Olympics so successful.

The Ever-Changing Olympics

Today's Olympic Games bear as little resemblance to those in 1896 as Olympiad I did to the contests in ancient Greece, when athletes competed in the nude, women were barred even as spectators, and victors received an olive branch as a symbol of victory. The Olympics have become a riveting drama in which more than 10,000 athletes from more than 170 nations compete in a festive pageant televised around the world.

Although founded on ancient athletic tradition, the modern Olympics have been in a state of perpetual evolution. Some changes have seemed arbitrary, as in 1908 when the marathon was lengthened from 25 miles to its now traditional 26 miles, 385 yards, a modification designed to allow the race to start at Windsor Castle, so the British royal family could watch. But most innovations have made the Games more meaningful and helped them adapt to changing times.

In 1896 there was one awards ceremony on the final day, with each winner receiving a silver medal and a crown of olive branches and each runner-up a bronze medal and a laurel crown. Today gold, silver, and bronze medals are handed out after every event, with the winners mounting a podium while the gold medalist's national anthem is played and his or her country's flag is raised.

Women first competed in 1900 in Paris; George Poage of the Milwaukee Athletic Club became the first African American to win a medal, taking third in the 400-meter hurdles in 1904; the first Winter Olympics were in 1924 in Chamonix, France; and the Olympics were first televised in 1936, when competition was beamed on an experimental basis to twenty-five theaters in Germany, the host country.

More recently, even the custom of holding the Summer and Winter Games in the same year was discarded: in 1994 the Winter Games were held in Lillehammer, Norway, only two years after the preceding Winter Olympics. The four-year interval between each Summer and Winter Olympics is maintained, but one of the Games is now held every two years.

The sports contested have also changed. Pentathlon, golf, croquet, swimming an obstacle course, and even live pigeon shooting have been replaced over the years by events like judo, volleyball, acrobatic skiing, and basketball, a sport that became a regular event in 1948.

The symbolism and pageantry that make the Olympics a unique competition have also evolved. The Olympic flag of five interlocking colored rings (blue, yellow, black, green, and red) on a white background first flew over the 1920 games in Antwerp, Belgium. Designed by de Coubertin, the banner symbolizes world unity because the flags of every nation contain at least one of those colors. Also debuting in Antwerp was the Olympic oath. Written by de Coubertin, it is read aloud during the opening ceremony by an athlete from the host country while holding a corner of the Olympic flag:

The modern Olympic Games bear little resemblance to the contests of ancient Greece when athletes competed in the nude.

In the name of all competitors, I promise that we shall take part in these Olympic Games, respecting and abiding by the rules which govern them, in the true spirit of sportsmanship, for the glory of sport and the honor of our teams.[8]

In 1928 a giant flame burned for the first time in Amsterdam, Holland, as a symbol of the original Olympics. Eight years later this flame was lit in Olympia, Greece, and carried to Berlin by runners bearing torches. In the 1956 Summer Olympics in Melbourne, Australia, athletes from every nation marched into the closing ceremony as one group instead of by country. Suggested by an Australian youth, John Ian Wing, this final march became another symbol of world unity.

Sportswriter Dick Schaap believes pageantry and symbolism have enabled the Olympics to transcend mere athletic competition:

The Olympics go beyond sports; they approach art. They offer ritual in the symbolic freeing of the pigeons, the solemn lighting of the Olympic flame, the quiet dignity of the Olympic oath. They offer competition with the animal excitement of physical combat, stamina against stamina, courage against courage. And, above all, they offer a singular spirit of a camaraderie born of shared victories, an understanding born of shared defeats.[9]

That spirit of camaraderie was important to de Coubertin, who believed goodwill created among athletes from various nations would help avoid future wars. Succeeding officials including Juan Antonio Samaranch, the Spaniard who in 1980 became president of the International Olympic Committee (IOC), also shared his dream: "Our philosophy [still] proceeds from the belief that sport is an inalienable part of the educational process and a factor for promoting peace, friendship, cooperation, and understanding among people."[10]

Although founded on lofty ideals, the Olympics through the years have sadly, even at times tragically, been interrupted or debased by war, diplomatic maneuvering, and brazen displays of nationalism and political ideology.

Politics Bedevil the Olympics

The ancient Olympics were so sacred that warring Greek states promised athletes safe passage through their territories so they could compete. But the modern world has shown no such respect: World War I forced cancellation of the 1916 Olympics and World War II the 1940 and 1944 Games.

In the second half of the twentieth century, many nations have boycotted the Olympics for a variety of political reasons. In 1980 the United States and sixty-one other nations refused to go to Moscow because the Soviet Union had invaded Afghanistan. Four years later, in retribution for the snub, the Soviet Union and thirteen of its allies sent no athletes to Los Angeles.

In 1936 Adolf Hitler used the Berlin Games to glorify Germany and to promote his twisted belief in Aryan superiority. Even though the performances of Jesse Owens and other African-American athletes shattered Hitler's racial myth, former IOC president Lord Killanin and John Rodda write in *The Olympic Games* that National Socialist (Nazi) propaganda tainted the Games:

> Sadly, though, the overall memory of the 1936 games was the "Deutschland über alles" [Germany above all others] atmosphere engendered by Hitler and the Nazis. Everywhere the eye was affronted by flag upon flag, bearing the crooked cross [the swastika], like so many weeds among the flower beds; everywhere the ear was assailed by loudspeakers playing martial music or the hysterical *Sieg Heil* [Hail victory] responses of the thoughtless multitudes to the appearance of [Hitler].[11]

When the Olympics resumed in 1948 following World War II, athletes from the United States and Soviet Union took their postwar enmity to London. Bob Mathias, a seventeen-year-old California high school student who won the first of his two gold medals in the decathlon, summed up this new athletic tension: "There were many more pressures on American athletes because of the Russians. They were in a sense the real enemy; you just loved to beat 'em. You just had to beat 'em. This feeling was strong down through the entire team."[12]

The 1968 Mexico City Olympics were marred by a different kind of politics—a protest against racism. After Tommie Smith won the 200-meter dash in a world record time of 19.8 seconds and teammate John Carlos finished third, the two African Americans stunned the world during the medal ceremony by raising clenched fists clad in black gloves. Smith explains the protest's symbolism:

> I wore a black right-hand glove and Carlos wore the left-hand glove of the same pair. My raised right hand stood

for the power in black America. Carlos's raised left hand stood for the unity of black America. Together they formed an arch of unity and power. The black scarf around my neck stood for black pride. The black socks with no shoes [they both wore] stood for black poverty in racist America. The totality of our effort was the regaining of black dignity.[13]

The Nazi flag is hoisted during the opening ceremony at the 1936 Olympics in Berlin. Hitler used the Olympics to showcase his belief in Aryan superiority.

And in the 1972 Olympics in Munich, Germany, eleven Israeli athletes were taken hostage by an Arab terrorist group and killed in a political act that horrified the world and violated everything the Olympics represent.

Amateurism

Perhaps the most dramatic change in the modern Olympics has been the death of one of its most sacred traditions—the amateur athlete. Only months after Jim Thorpe won two gold medals in 1912, the IOC took them away upon discovering that the great Native American athlete had played semiprofessional baseball. And Paavo Nurmi was barred from the 1932 Olympics for allegedly having

Tommie Smith (left) and John Carlos (right) raised clenched fists at the 1968 Mexico City Olympics as a symbolic protest against racism.

kept $100 in expense money after a competition in Germany. Yet just sixty years later in the 1992 Olympics in Barcelona, Spain, the gold medal in basketball was won by the United States "Dream Team," led by Chicago Bulls star Michael Jordan. Jordan and all his teammates were full-time professionals, earning millions of dollars a year.

How could Olympic rules of eligibility have changed so quickly?

Olympic historian David Wallechinsky states that the Olympic ideal of the amateur athlete was distorted from its inception:

> The concept of amateurism actually developed in nineteenth-century England as a means of preventing the working classes from competing against the aristocracy. The wealthy could take part in sports without worrying about having to make a living, and thus could pursue the ideal of amateurism.[14]

In *All That Glitters Is Not Gold*, William O. Johnson Jr. claims that even ancient Greek athletes were not true amateurs: "Many athletes were paid outright by their hometowns and won prizes of oxen and drachmas [Greek money]. The famed Theagenes won more than fourteen-hundred prizes in boxing, running, and [other events]."[15]

Jesse Owens, who turned professional after the 1936 Olympics, summed up the problem poor athletes faced in sacrificing their lives to compete: "I had four gold medals, but you can't eat four gold medals."[16] The vast majority of Olympic athletes have never made any money from their sports, but as commercial opportunities for some stars began to emerge in the twentieth century, it became difficult to define who was an amateur.

In the 1960s and 1970s, companies began making secret payments to athletes like Jean-Claude Killy to endorse products. The Soviet Union gave its athletes government jobs that allowed them to train full time and rewarded them for winning medals. Vasily Alexeyev supposedly had a job as a mining engineer, but he never did anything except lift weights.

When many people began to ask whether such athletes were not really "professionals" because they made their living from sports, Olympic officials were compelled to rewrite the eligiblity rules.

In 1971 the IOC replaced the word "amateur" in its charter with the term "eligible athlete" and gave the international organizations governing each sport the right to define that term. In 1972 the IOC allowed athletes to receive several types of financial support, including payments from the IOC itself, to subsidize their training. Though the changes made it possible for a few track stars, skiers, and figure skaters to earn large sums of money, the vast majority of Olympic athletes still receive so little money that they have to work to support themselves.

The changes blurred the lines between "amateur" and "professional" so greatly that in 1988 the federation that regulated tennis allowed professionals to compete in Seoul, Korea. Tennis professionals were soon followed by pro basketball and hockey players, and major league baseball players will be eligible for the first time for the 2002 Summer Games in Sydney, Australia.

These professional athletes are now considered amateurs in the Olympics because they compete in the Games for free. Historian John Lucas believes the new standard of eligibility is more pragmatic:

> The rules have changed. The Olympic Games are not looking for amateurs, but for those possessing the elusive "amateur spirit," a certain mind-set wherein the profit motive does not dominate all other motives, a thought process in which the individual perceives himself or herself as being more in love with the enterprise for its own sake than for the money involved. Because there is no way to read minds, to tell one kind of athlete from the others, past IOC President

Lord Killanin and now [Juan Antonio] Samaranch have invited them *all* into the Olympic arena: An amateur athlete is anyone who honestly considers himself or herself to be one.[17]

Olympic Commercialism

Athletes, however, are not the only ones involved in the Olympics who have been swayed by money. Olympiad I in 1896 was financed by the sale of stamps and medals and by a gift from Greek architect Georgios Averoff valued at over $100,000.

But a century later the 1996 Summer Olympics in Atlanta, Georgia, cost an estimated $1.5 billion. The Olympics have become big business, and the IOC, whose members are elected by associations in competing nations, have been forced to embrace commercialism to finance the Games.

The main source of Olympic revenue is television fees, which have grown explosively since the Columbia Broadcasting System (CBS) paid $50,000 to televise the 1960 Winter Games in Squaw Valley, California. Fees for Summer Games, which are generally more popular, climbed to $25 million in 1976, $85 million in 1980, $225 million in 1984, and more than $400 million in 1992—sums representing only television rights in America.

Today's Olympic Games are big business. Here, a vendor sells T-shirts and other Olympic souvenirs during the 1996 Atlanta Games.

Sites of the Olympic Games

Year	Summer	Winter
1896	Athens, Greece	Not held
1900	Paris, France	Not held
1904	St. Louis, MO	Not held
1908	London, England	Not held
1912	Stockholm, Sweden	Not held
1916	Not held	Not held
1920	Antwerp, Belgium	Not held
1924	Paris, France	Chamonix, France
1928	Amsterdam, the Netherlands	St. Moritz, Switzerland
1932	Los Angeles, CA	Lake Placid, NY
1936	Berlin, Germany	Garmisch-Partenkirchen, Germany
1940	Not held	Not held
1944	Not held	Not held
1948	London, England	St. Moritz, Switzerland
1952	Helsinki, Finland	Oslo, Norway
1956	Melbourne, Australia	Cortina, Italy
1960	Rome, Italy	Squaw Valley, CA
1964	Tokyo, Japan	Innsbruck, Austria
1968	Mexico City, Mexico	Grenoble, France
1972	Munich, West Germany	Sapporo, Japan
1976	Montreal, Canada	Innsbruck, Austria
1980	Moscow, Soviet Union	Lake Placid, NY
1984	Los Angeles, CA	Sarajevo, Yugoslavia
1988	Seoul, South Korea	Calgary, Canada
1992	Barcelona, Spain	Albertville, France
1994		Lillehammer, Norway
1996	Atlanta, GA	
1998		Nagano, Japan
2000	Sydney, Australia	
2002		Salt Lake City, UT

Olympic commercialization escalated after the 1976 Summer Games saddled Montreal, Canada, with a debt of $1 billion. Because IOC rules say the host country must pay all debts arising from the Olympics, the future of the Games was in doubt: What country would want to go into debt to host them?

But when Peter Ueberroth chaired the Los Angeles Olympic Organizing Committee for the 1984 Summer Games, he capitalized on the money making potential of the popular events. Olympic officials had always courted sponsors, who paid small sums for the right to be associated with the Olympics. Ueberroth, however, upped the ante by limiting the number of official sponsors to thirty. For example, Coca-Cola paid $12.6 million to advertise itself as the "official soft drink" of the Games, and the 1984 Olympics made a profit of nearly $223 million.

More Money

In *The Olympics at 100,* Associated Press sports editor Larry Siddons admits, "At times it feels as if 'Richer, richer, richer' has replaced 'Citius, altius, fortius' as the Olympic theme."[18] The opportunity to make even more money, Siddons claims, was the reason the IOC decided to start alternating the Summer and Winter Olympics every two years:

> Having discovered the sweet smell of cash in Los Angeles, the IOC looked for ways to ease more money out of [the Olympics] and it found the answer in the calendar. Nothing in the rules said Summer and Winter Games had to be in the same year. It was a tradition, but the IOC had found that tradition doesn't pay the bills. It was time for a change.[19]

But Siddons notes that IOC officials claim the future of the Olympics would have been endangered if they had not found new ways to increase revenue.

When nations realized that an Olympics could provide them with an economic boost, the battle to host the Games intensified and in 1998 led to the biggest scandal in Olympic history. An investigation revealed that a handful of IOC members had accepted, and in some cases requested, money and lavish gifts from the Salt Lake City (Utah) Olympic Planning Committee for their vote to award that city the 2002 Winter Games.

The result in 1999 was the resignation of three IOC directors, the dismissal of nine more members, changes in procedure to prevent future problems, and lingering questions about the honesty of a movement founded on high ideals.

The Olympics Are Still Golden

But in *All That Glitters Is Not Gold,* William O. Johnson Jr. writes that despite any problems they have suffered through the years, the Olympics have always retained the power and grandeur to capture the imagination of the world:

The Olympics is not only a matter of profit motives and movie careers and beer commercials and box scores kept by nationalists. The Olympic Games are also the stuff from which dreams are made. The feats of Olympians can cast a spell for decades. They bring reveries to little boys lying abed in the twilight of summer evenings, and they offer a precious chance for open admiration and genuine wonder among grown men.[20]

CHAPTER 2

Jim Thorpe: The Most Tragic Olympic Champion

The sun rose May 28, 1888, a fiery yellow ball casting a luminous glow on the dirt path leading to a small, two-room cabin in the Oklahoma Territory. To Charlotte View Thorpe, the golden rays were inspiration for a Native American name for her newborn son: Wa-tho-huck, meaning "bright path."

The "path" James Francis Thorpe took was, indeed, "bright": he was a star in college sports, an Olympic champion, major league baseball player, and Hall of Fame pioneer in professional football. But his journey was also filled with darkness: the deaths of both his twin brother and his first-born son, the loss of his Olympic medals, and a long descent into alcoholism and poverty when his days as a sports star ended.

"I cannot decide," Thorpe once said, "whether I was well named or not. Many a time the path has beamed bright for me, but just as often it has been dark and bitter indeed."[21]

Growing Up

In 1878 Hiram Thorpe moved from the Sac and Fox reservation in Iowa to Oklahoma Territory— Oklahoma did not become a state until 1907—and began raising crops, horses, cattle, and chickens

Hiram Thorpe, Jim Thorpe's grandfather and son of Chief Black Hawk.

on a 160-acre farm located near what is now Prague, Oklahoma. Known as "Big Hiram" for his size and strength, he was the area's best swimmer, wrestler, and rider. Like his father, Jim Thorpe resembled his famous great-grandfather, Chief Black Hawk, who in 1832 led the Sac and Fox in the war that bears his name.

Charlotte, of Potawatomi and Kickapoo ancestry, was Thorpe's third wife; he had already fathered several children by the time Jim and his twin brother, Charles, were born. The boys had daily chores, including capturing and taming wild horses and hunting game. But Thorpe wrote lovingly of his childhood and the games that helped build the muscle, coordination, and stamina that would make him famous.

> Up to the time little Charlie died at the age of eight of pneumonia, we roamed the prairies and played together always. Our lives were lived in the open, winter and summer. And we played hard. Our favorite game was "Follow the Leader." Depending on the "leader," that can be an exciting game. Many a time in following I had to swim rivers, climb trees, and run under horses. But our favorite was climbing hickory or tall cedar trees, getting on the top, swinging there and leaping to the ground ready for the next "follow."[22]

When the twins were six, they began attending an Indian Agency school twenty-five miles away. A disinterested student, Jim became lonesome after the death of his brother and one morning simply left the school, jogging all the way home. An angry Hiram Thorpe hitched horses to his wagon and drove Jim back to school, only to have his stubborn son run away again minutes later. Jim even beat his father home.

Thorpe Goes to Carlisle

In June 1904, when the sixteen-year-old Thorpe began attending Carlisle (Pennsylvania) Indian School, a trade school that also offered basic educational courses, he was only 5 feet 5 1/2 inches tall and weighed 115 pounds. Thorpe became an apprentice tailor and worked part time in the community, cooking and cleaning house for $5 a month, with half his earnings going to Carlisle.

Because he was small, Thorpe played football in a shop league on the tailor's team, not the varsity team that famed Coach Glenn "Pop" Warner led against the nation's top college teams. Warner, who later coached at Cornell, the University of Georgia, and the University of Pittsburgh, said Carlisle athletes had "a real race pride and a fierce determination to show the palefaces what they could do when the odds were even."[23]

In the spring of 1907 while cleaning up near the school's track, Thorpe watched with amusement as a long line of athletes failed to clear a high jump bar set at 5 feet 9 inches. Now 6 feet tall and strong, Thorpe said, "That don't seem very high." When Warner asked if Thorpe had ever high-jumped, he responded, "Not over a bar. But if a horse can do it, I can do it."[24] Thorpe rolled up his heavy work overalls, took off his shoes, and with a burst of speed and soaring leap cleared the bar by several inches.

Thorpe became a star in track and football and competed in baseball, lacrosse, basketball, hockey, and other sports. What amazed Warner was Thorpe's ability to master anything physical—he even became a collegiate ballroom dancing champion.

Thorpe Becomes a Star

A 1909 dual meet in Easton, Pennsylvania, showed how dominating Thorpe was. Lafayette College students who welcomed the visiting team were amazed when only five young men arrived. "Is this your entire team?" a student asked. "Well, no," said Thorpe. "The little fellow over there is just the manager."[25] Carlisle beat the forty-six-player Lafayette squad 71–41 as Thorpe finished third in the 100-yard dash and won the 120-yard hurdles, 220-yard low hurdles, broad jump, high jump, shot put, and discus.

Thorpe (back row, fourth from left) on the Carlisle Indian School track team in 1909.

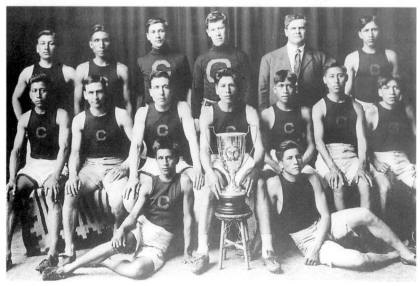

27

Tiring of school, Thorpe left Carlisle after the 1909 track season. After a brief trip back home he headed east with friends and played baseball for money, a decision that would later cost him his Olympic medals:

> A couple of Carlisle baseball players named Jesse Young Deer and Joe Libby were going to North Carolina to play ball, so I tagged along just for the trip. [They] were fair

Thorpe was an All-American halfback in 1911 and 1912.

outfielders, and they caught on with the Rocky Mount club. I got short of money, so when the manager offered me fifteen dollars a week to play third base, I took it.[26]

Thorpe also pitched, winning nine games and losing ten. He went home for the winter but the next spring played for Fayetteville in the Eastern Carolina Association as a pitcher and first baseman.

Thorpe returned to Carlisle in 1911 after Warner convinced him he could make the 1912 Olympic team. Twenty-three years old and in his athletic prime, Thorpe became a national sports sensation.

An All-American halfback in 1911 and 1912, Thorpe led Carlisle to victories over the nation's best teams. In an 18–15 victory in 1911 over defending national champion Harvard, Thorpe kicked four field goals, ran for a touchdown, and was a defensive stalwart. Commented Harvard Coach Percy Haughton: "Watching him turn the ends, slash off tackle, kick and pass and tackle, I realized that here was the theoretical super player in flesh and blood."[27]

Thorpe Is Golden in Stockholm

However, even Warner wondered if Thorpe's dazzling athletic ability was enough to win two gold medals. "I know you're strong," Warner said, "but do you think you have the endurance to go all out in five events [the pentathlon], then come back and take on ten events?" Thorpe replied, "I know I can win enough of them to bring back two gold medals."[28]

On June 14, 1912, Thorpe, Warner, and classmate Louis Tewanima, who would finish second in the 10,000-meter run, set sail for Stockholm, Sweden. During the voyage, the athletes kept in shape on a cork track that circled the *SS Finland*. Some accounts claim Thorpe slept the trip away but Ralph Craig, gold medalist in the 100-meter and 200-meter dashes, said Thorpe trained hard: "I remember running laps and doing calisthenics with Jim every day on the ship."[29]

At 6 feet 1 inch and 181 pounds, Thorpe was an imposing figure. His lean, muscular frame was topped by a 40-inch chest that tapered to a 32-inch waist. His legs were lean and sinewy. But it was Thorpe's fierce will to win that would carry him through the grueling challenge of fifteen events.

The pentathlon, no longer contested after 1924, was July 7. Thorpe won the long jump with a leap of 23 feet 2.7 inches, finished third in the javelin with a throw of 153 feet 2 19/20 inches,

and won the 200-meter run in 22.90 seconds. Thorpe then won the discus with a throw of 116 feet 8.1 inches, 3 feet farther than teammate Avery Brundage, who later (from 1952 to 1972) would reign as president of the International Olympic Committee. The final event was the 1,500-meter event, a race just short of a mile that Thorpe won in 4:44.80. Thorpe's low score of 7 (based on finishes in each event; 1 point for first, 2 for second, and so forth) was a third of the 21 points Norway's Ferdinand Bie totaled to win silver.

The three-day decathlon competition began July 13. Thorpe finished second in the 100-meter

Thorpe training aboard a ship on his way to the 1912 Olympics (top) where he competed in the 1,500-meter (bottom, second from left).

dash and long jump but won the shot put with a toss of 42 feet 5
9/20 inches. The next day Thorpe won the high jump with a leap
of 6 feet 1.6 inches, finished second in the 400-meter run, and captured the 110-meter hurdles in 15.6 seconds, an Olympic decathlon record unbroken for four decades.

On the final day Thorpe was second in the discus and third in
the pole vault and javelin, leaving just one event, the 1,500 meters.
Coming at the end of the decathlon, the race is often one of mere
survival for weary competitors. But Thorpe's raw power and endurance propelled him to victory in 4:40.1 minutes, 4 seconds
faster than he had ever run that distance. He totaled 8,412.995
points, over 700 more than Hugo Wieslander of Sweden. Decathlon points are based on the results in each event.

When King Gustav V of Sweden awarded Thorpe his gold
medals, he said, "Sir, you are the greatest athlete in the world."
Thorpe responded simply, "Thanks, king."[30] It was an ultimate
compliment that would forever be linked to his name.

Cruel Aftermath of the Olympics

Thorpe returned home to a hero's welcome, including a parade in
New York where more than a million people cheered him. "I
heard people yelling my name and I couldn't realize how one fellow could have so many friends," he said.[31]

Turning down offers of thousands of dollars for personal appearances, Thorpe returned to Carlisle and played football, scoring 25 touchdowns and setting a national collegiate record with
198 points. In a 27–6 victory over powerful West Point, Thorpe
scored 22 points. In one brilliant play, he ran a punt back 95 yards
for a touchdown. Army halfback Dwight D. Eisenhower, a future
president, said of Thorpe, "On the football field, there was no one
like him in the world."[32]

But in early 1913 Roy Johnson of the *Worcester* (Massachusetts)
Telegram reported that Thorpe had played baseball for money. In
the uproar that followed, Thorpe, who in New York had wondered
at his many friends, appealed for mercy from the Amateur Athletic
Union (AAU), the organization that determined eligibility:

> I hope I will be partly excused by the fact that I was sim-
> ply an Indian schoolboy and did not know all about such
> things. In fact I did not know that I was doing wrong be-
> cause I was doing what I knew several other college men
> had done except that they did not use their own names [as
> members of the pro teams]. I have received offers amount-
> ing to thousands of dollars since my victories last summer,

but I have turned them all down because I did not care to make money from my athletic skill. I hope [sports officials] and the people will not be too hard in judging me.[33]

The public generally backed Thorpe but AAU and Olympic officials made him return his medals and $50,000 in gifts, including a jewel-encrusted Viking ship from the czar of Russia. Chief Meyers, a teammate in professional baseball, said the losses devastated Thorpe:

> I remember, very late one night, Jim came in and woke me up. I remember it like it was only last night. He was crying and tears were rolling down his cheeks. "You know, Chief," he said. "The king of Sweden gave me those trophies, he gave them to me. But they took them away from me. They're mine, Chief, I won them fair and square." It broke his heart and he never fully recovered.[34]

Pro Baseball

The New York Giants in 1913 signed Thorpe to play baseball for $5,000. It was a huge sum at the time, but manager John McGraw ruthlessly admitted he wanted Thorpe to attract fans: "They'll pay just to see the big Indian take batting practice."[35]

Thorpe's six-year major league career was not a great one. Never a starter on a regular basis, his batting average was .252 in 289 games from 1913 to 1919. In 1916 he was demoted to the minor leagues and played with the Milwaukee Brewers of the American Association, batting .274 and stealing a league-leading 48 bases to earn a trip back to the Giants.

In 1913 Thorpe married Iva Miller, who he had met at Carlisle, and two years later they had a son, Jim Thorpe Jr. The boy died in 1918 from infantile paralysis, and Al Schacht, a Giants pitcher, said Thorpe was never the same after that. He became silent and withdrawn, missed practices, and often did not seem to care about baseball.

Thorpe's relationship with McGraw, never congenial, exploded in 1918 when the notoriously hot-tempered manager, provoked by a base-running mistake, called Thorpe a "dumb Indian." Thorpe chased McGraw all over the Polo Grounds, the Giants' home field, and it took half the team to restrain him. McGraw released him the next year after two games, claiming Thorpe could not hit a curve ball. But Thorpe, who finished 1919 with the Boston Braves and hit .327 in sixty games, said that was a lie. In 1951 he told the *Milwaukee Journal*:

They said I couldn't hit a curve ball. One day John Mc-Graw said, "Let me see you hit the guy who's pitching out there for the Phillies." I hit a curve against the fence in right field for two bases. When asked who the pitcher was, Thorpe smiled, answering, "A guy named Alexander"—Grover Cleveland Alexander [a Hall of Fame pitcher with an excellent curve].[36]

Thorpe played minor league baseball until 1928, when he retired with a .320 average in more than 700 minor league games.

Thorpe holding his son James Francis Jr., who died from infantile paralysis.

Pro Football Pioneer

In 1915 Thorpe also began playing football with the Canton (Ohio) Bulldogs for $250 a game. He became the biggest star of pro football's early years and in 1920 was named the first president of the American Professional Football Association, which later became the National Football League (NFL). It was a nonpaying job with few duties; the league, like baseball's McGraw, was taking advantage of Thorpe's fame. But Thorpe helped popularize pro football and in 1963 was a charter member of the NFL Hall of Fame.

Between 1915 and 1929 Thorpe played for more than a half-dozen teams, finishing his career at age forty-one with the Chicago Cardinals. He headed a team called the Oorang Indians, a squad of Native American players who competed in 1922 and 1923. Ed Healy, a tackle for the Chicago Bears in the 1920s, said Thorpe was the best he ever played against:

I had seen Thorpe perform for the Carlisle Indians against the Springfield YMCA [team] in 1912, and I played against him in pro ball. Mr. Thorpe could hurt you both offensively and defensively. When he was in shape, he could go sixty minutes at top clip. He was the best in my era, without question.[37]

As a football sensation, Thorpe was named the first president of the American Professional Football Association, which later became the NFL.

Thorpe, however, was often not in "shape" because of age, poor training habits, and a drinking problem that first surfaced at the Olympics. Dan Ferris, a former president of the AAU, said that after winning the decathlon Thorpe got so drunk that "when King Gustav sent a cutter out to our boat to pick up Thorpe, we had to tell them [he] was not on board."[38]

Disastrous Private Life

Thorpe's drinking and vagabond lifestyle as a pro athlete took him away from home constantly, contributing in 1923 to the breakup of his first marriage, which had produced three daughters—Gail, Charlotte, and Grace. Two years later Thorpe married Freeda Kirkpatrick and they had four sons—Carl Philip, William, Richard, and John. The marriage lasted until 1941, when the couple divorced.

When his athletic career ended, Thorpe spent two decades drifting around the country. His athletic fame won him jobs officiating at dance marathons and wrestling matches and bit parts in movies, but manual labor was often the only work Thorpe could find.

When the Olympics came to Los Angeles in 1932, Thorpe was there not as an honored guest but as a laborer, digging the foundation for a hospital for $4 a day. When U.S. Vice President Charles Curtis, also of Native American descent, heard that Thorpe did not have enough money for a ticket, he invited the one-time Olympic champion to sit with him.

A Quiet End

During World War II, Thorpe worked in a defense plant in Dearborn, Michigan, and served briefly in the Merchant Marine. In 1945 he married Patricia Askew. Thorpe had always spoken without charge to schools and charitable organizations about his Olympic experience and Native American heritage. When his new wife convinced him that he should be paid for those appearances, Thorpe began making a modest living.

Some of his old glory was restored in 1950 when the Associated Press named him the greatest athlete of the first half-century. Famous again, Thorpe told reporters only one thing would make him happy: "In the twilight of my life the one thing I dream of constantly is that the American people will try to get back for me the Olympic trophies I won in 1912. I'd be the happiest man in the world if I could just get my medals back."[39]

The "greatest athlete in the world" died March 28, 1953, at age sixty-five after suffering a heart attack while eating dinner with his wife in their trailer home in Lomita, California. State officials in Oklahoma refused to pay for a monument for his grave, but Pennsylvania communities of Mauch Chunk and East Mauch Chunk voted to honor him by merging under his name. He was buried in

Jim Thorpe, Pennsylvania, in February 1954, his grave graced by a red granite memorial engraved with King Gustav's famous commendation.

Redemption

Jim Thorpe died without his medals. But a long fight that began in 1945, when the Oklahoma Legislature asked the AAU to restore his records, picked up speed after his death. The AAU and IOC finally relented, and on October 13, 1982, Thorpe was reinstated as the 1912 pentathlon and decathlon champion. New medals were cast and given to all of his seven children.

Thorpe's path had brightened one last time.

CHAPTER 3

Paavo Nurmi:
Winning with "Sisu"

Paavo Nurmi of Finland earned the nickname "the Flying Finn" for the grace and ease with which he ran to victory after victory. In a dozen races in three Olympics, Nurmi won nine gold medals and three silver, including a then-record five gold medals in 1924. Nurmi also set more than thirty world outdoor and many indoor records at distances ranging from 1,500 meters (the metric mile) to 20,000 meters, a virtuosity never seen before or since in the sport of running.

Although "Flying Finn" perfectly described his effortless stride, the nickname seemed inadequate to describe this remarkable runner. Nurmi's superiority was so amazing that the world began to wonder about the source of his power. Was it due to a diet of the Finnish favorites black bread and fish? Was it because his heart beat only forty times a minute? Did Nurmi's strange habit of timing himself during races with a stopwatch help him to victory? And why had Finland produced so many other great runners like Hannes Kolehmainen, who in 1912 won three gold medals?

In his 1927 book *The Athletic Finn*, K. P. Silberg tried to explain the Finnish phenomenon. He claimed that Finnish runners were successful in distance races because they shared an attitude of stoicism and mental toughness revered in their homeland:

> There is a certain quality which the Finns respect most profoundly in a man. This quality is expressed in their language by the word *sisu*. "Suomalainen sisu"—"Finnish sisu"—is a proverbial expression among the Finns. There is no exact equivalent in our language for this word—endurance, stamina, perseverance, grit, are words that most nearly correspond to it in English. It denotes a determined and co-extensive effort of mind and body to consummate a difficult task in the face of the most formidable odds.

And, in our opinion, it is this quality, combined with a naturally strong physique, that brings the Finns their athletic victories.[40]

A Difficult Childhood

Paavo Nurmi was born June 13, 1897, in Turku, a seaport in southwest Finland. The son of a carpenter who died when Nurmi was twelve, the future runner grew up bitterly poor. His mother became a laundress; and Paavo, the eldest of five children, had to quit school and work to help support the family. He became an errand runner, making deliveries by pushing a heavy wheelbarrow through the streets of his hometown.

As a young boy Paavo Nurmi enjoyed running in the pine forests that surrounded Turku. As he grew older, running became a form of mental and emotional release for a lonely young man. A friend once said "running was the replacement for his father. Running was Nurmi's attempt at finding real life."[41] In *Great Olympic Champions,* John Devaney describes the joy with which Nurmi ran:

> Puffing smoke high into the icy blue sky, the morning train rattled toward the tiny town in western Finland on a cold winter morning. The engineer of the train waved at the small boy running along the tracks. "Run faster," he shouted. "This morning I'm going to beat you to the station." The boy grinned. And then he ran faster, his legs stretching out. Slowly he began to move ahead of the train, running with the flowing grace of a mountain deer. When the train chugged into the station, the boy was already there, standing on the platform, hands on hips, a big smile across his face.[42]

Nurmi's life was given a purpose in 1912 when Hannes Kolehmainen won the 5,000-meter and 10,000-meter races and the 8,000-meter cross-country run in the Summer Olympics in Sweden. Kolehmainen became his idol and he vowed to win a gold medal himself. Nurmi began competing for Turun Urheiluliitto, a local sports club, winning his first race at age seventeen with a time of just over 5 minutes for 1,500 meters. It was a fine race for a teenager, but the victorious Nurmi was unhappy because his time was more than a minute slower than the Olympic record.

A military courier during World War I, Nurmi continued to train by getting up before reveille to run mile after mile. In early 1918 Nurmi entered and won a 20,000-meter race for civilians

After winning the 5,000- and 10,000-meter races in the 1912 Olympics in Sweden, Hannes Kolehmainen (taking the gold) became an inspiration for Paavo Nurmi.

while wearing his uniform, carrying his rifle, and wearing a heavy backpack. Race officials were so surprised to see Nurmi win in military gear that they thought he had cheated by taking a short-cut; they eventually realized he had won fairly despite his self-imposed handicap.

In 1918, after the war ended, Nurmi returned to Turku and worked in an architectural office. The next Olympics were only two years away and he began to devote himself to winning a gold medal, running 100 miles or more each week. Although many runners today train that hard, such demanding workouts were un-heard of in Nurmi's era. The grueling workouts, however, gave Nurmi the strength and endurance to win.

The little boy who once raced trains now began to run against the ultimate opponent: time itself. Vernon Morgan, who com-peted against Nurmi in the 1928 Olympics and was sports editor of the Reuters news service for three decades, explains Nurmi's unique training habit:

> Nurmi was as ahead of his time in his thinking about run-ning as he was in the quality and quantity of his training and he realized that an even race was an essential in long-distance running. So he carried a watch in his left hand

during training and competition. I'll never forget his annoyance when in the 3,000-meter steeplechase in Amsterdam in 1928 [in which I also took part] he fell in the water jump and damaged his watch. He would never say whether this cost him the race, in which he finished second to his teammate Toivo Loukola.[43]

Nurmi trained scientifically, recording times for all his workouts and devising race strategies based on how fast he could run. He calculated overall times for each race and how fast to run each lap around the track to win. Nurmi trained hard so he could meet the times he set, consulting his watch during races to stay on schedule.

The 1920 Olympics

The 1920 Olympics in Antwerp, Belgium, were the first since 1912 because the Games had been suspended during World War I. Eight years after starring in Stockholm, Kolehmainen won gold in the marathon. But he was upstaged by Nurmi, who won three gold medals and a silver.

Nurmi's first race was a disappointment. On August 17 he lost the 5,000-meter event to Joseph Guillemot of France, but learned a vital lesson about race tactics. Nurmi had been so determined to win that he had ignored his race schedule and immediately shot to the lead, with Guillemot right behind. Nurmi led until near the end when Guillemot, with a strong finish, passed him to win in 14:55.6, almost 5 seconds faster than Nurmi. The victory was amazing because the Frenchman during World War I had been exposed to poison gas, which weakened his lungs so much that doctors predicted he would never run again.

Realizing he had made a mistake by allowing another runner to set the pace, Nurmi was more cautious three days later in the 10,000 meters, allowing James Wilson of Scotland to take the lead. With two laps to go, Nurmi dashed to the front, only to have Guillemot pass him again in the backstretch of the final lap. But this time Nurmi, who had raced the way he wanted to, had enough energy left to overtake the Frenchman and win by eight yards in 31:45.8, more than a minute faster than he had ever run that distance.

His first victory proved to be his most unpleasant, however, for Guillemot threw up on his shoes after the finish. Unaware that the start time had been moved up by several hours, Guillemot had eaten a large lunch shortly before the race. Nurmi, as he would after other victories, calmly walked off the track, showing no trace of emotion.

Nurmi capped his first Olympics August 23 with a double victory in cross-country. He captured an individual gold medal for finishing first over the 8,000-meter course and a team gold medal for helping the Finnish team win.

The 1924 Olympics

Four years later in Paris, Nurmi was at his greatest. He won the 1,500-meter and 5,000-meter races, the 10,000-meter cross-country run, and the 3,000-meter team cross-country race. Nurmi won five gold medals, taking both individual gold and team gold medals in the longer cross-country race.

Nurmi's most amazing performance came July 10, an insufferably hot day in which he earned his reputation as a superman by winning two gold medals in just two hours. Even though Nurmi eased up to save energy for the 5,000-meter race, he won the 1,500 meters in 3:53.6, an Olympic record that was just a second slower than the world record.

In the 5,000-meter race, run only a half-hour after his first victory, Nurmi faced a stiff challenge from Finlander Ville Ritola, a rival Nurmi disliked who had already won gold medals in the 10,000-meter race and the 3,000-meter steeplechase. After a fierce battle in which Ritola sped out to an early lead, forcing Nurmi to

Nurmi competes in the 1,500-meter race in the 1924 Paris Olympics, where he won five gold medals.

chase him and scrap his timetable, Nurmi surged ahead at the end to beat Ritola by two-tenths of a second in 14:31.2. This is how a Finnish writer described the dramatic finish:

> At the 4,500-meter mark Nurmi is still ahead. It is now the last lap. Nurmi is increasing his speed consistently, but Ritola is relentless. The end is approaching. What! Ritola is now abreast of Nurmi? The spectators are amazed. It is inconceivable. A few tense moments as the titans battle. But the tension is soon relieved: Nurmi is Nurmi. A quick glance about him, and the situation is changed; a few faster leaping strides and the intervening distance [between runners] is two meters. Nurmi arrives at the tape entirely composed and confident, with Ritola only a meter behind him.[44]

But Nurmi's series of superhuman performances was not yet over. The weather in Paris had been unbearably hot and muggy, and the temperature hit 100 degrees July 12 for the cross-country race. The runners started in the stadium, racing out into the hills surrounding Paris before returning for a final lap. Eight runners collapsed and needed to be hospitalized, and only fifteen of thirty-eight starters finished.

In 100-degree weather, Nurmi finished first in the 3,000-meter team cross-country race where only fifteen of thirty-eight starters finished.

But Nurmi, with Ritola once again chasing him, trotted serenely back into the stadium to win the individual gold medal and share the team gold. "He looks," one writer said, "as though ice water were being pumped through his veins."[45] Marveling at his awe-inspiring constitution, people began referring to Nurmi as a "frankenstein created to annihilate time" and a "running machine." The next day, with many cross-country runners still recovering, Nurmi finished first in the 3,000-meter team cross-country race.

It was Nurmi's powerful mental attitude of *sisu* that enabled him to run to victory despite steamy weather, his rivals, and the agony of his own body during competition. Nurmi once said "mind is everything: muscles—a piece of rubber"; another time he stated, "All that I am, I am because of my mind."[46] This was the real secret of his success.

Nurmi's Personality

In 1925 Nurmi visited the United States, winning all but one of fifty-five races he ran and making more fans than ever. In a radio address during his three-month tour, Nurmi explained his racing philosophy:

> My greetings to the youths of this country are, that they practice athletics on principle, without expecting immediate rewards. One must learn to win modestly, and to lose with good spirit. This indeed is the mark of a true athlete. Above all, one must never be concerned about rewards. In a race always follow your own plan, and be not concerned about your rivals, whether they are ahead of you or behind you. This is my greeting and my advice to my young American friends.[47]

Nurmi, however, was not always as high-minded as those comments indicate. During the tour, Nurmi accepted thousands of dollars in appearance fees, along with sixty gold medals, three gold watches, and twelve new suits.

Although he was one of the biggest sports stars of his era, Nurmi was not well-liked by his opponents or by the news media. Never a gracious winner, when Ritola stuck out his hand after their brilliant duel in the 5,000-meter race, Nurmi just stared at it, looked into Ritola's eyes briefly, and turned away.

Reporters always expect to be welcomed by sports stars because the stories they write are, after all, free publicity for athletes. But in *The Athletic Finn*, Silberg comments on Nurmi's disdain of the media:

> He is not communicative enough to satisfy our newspaper writers. He remarked repeatedly to his friends that he cannot see why people should be interested in anything in him beyond his running. He avoids publicity like a pestilence. And [famed sportswriter] Paul Gallico wrote in his column in the *Chicago Daily News*: "Hang it all, Nurmi hasn't been quite overwritten yet. The very way the man seems to hate reporters and cameramen is good for plenty of copy.

Mr. Nurmi not only says he doesn't want to be picture-graphed and interviewed, but he means it and runs from the representatives of the press as though Old Nick were after him. What on earth is the matter with the man? Ain't he human?"[48]

Nurmi's Final Gold Medal

At the 1928 Olympics in Amsterdam, Holland, Nurmi was thirty-one and had lost some of his speed and endurance. The 10,000-meter race was held on the opening day, July 29, and Nurmi edged Ritola by one-tenth of a second in an Olympic record time of 30:18.8.

On August 3 his archrival, Ritola, beat him for the gold in the 5,000-meter race by two hundredths of a second. The next day Nurmi took silver again in the steeplechase, a 3,000-meter race that involves running and jumping over water obstacles, with a time of 9:31.2. The winner was teammate Toivo Loukola.

Like his idol Kolehmainen, Nurmi wanted to end his Olympic career with a marathon victory. He set a record for a marathon in 1932; but, on the eve of the Olympics in Los Angeles, a German official claimed Nurmi had kept $100 in expense money after a race, causing Olympic officials to revoke the runner's amateur status. Nurmi denied the charge and went to Los Angeles to appeal the ruling, but he failed and his Olympic career was over.

One More Olympic Run

Although Nurmi became wealthy with a clothing store and real estate investments, he was even more reclusive and morose in retirement than while competing. A friend once tried to defend the taciturn Nurmi: "He is silent with people he doesn't know, as always. But I don't think he is bitter. He just leads his own life."[49]

Nurmi, though, would have one more moment of glory. When the Olympic Games came to Helsinki, Finland, in 1952, he carried the Olympic torch into the stadium and handed it to Kolehmainen, who lit the Olympic flame. Nurmi trained for the short run so he would look good before thousands of cheering fans, who on their way into the stadium passed a life-sized bronze statute of Nurmi.

But those cheers were one of the few human bright spots in Nurmi's lonely post-Olympic existence. Nurmi married briefly and fathered a son, but he divorced his wife after one year and was never close to his only child.

Several years before Nurmi's death on October 2, 1974, Olympic historian Johnson wrote: "In Helsinki, where he lives in an apartment building which he owns himself, Nurmi is considered to be a miser, a sour and penny-pinching fellow who made a fortune. He was certainly worshipped and envied, but perhaps rarely loved."[50]

Nurmi wanted to end his career with a marathon victory, but his amateur status was revoked at the 1932 Olympics in Los Angeles for previously keeping $100 in expense money.

When he died, Nurmi left his estate to an institute that re-searched heart disease, an illness he suffered in his later years. In a rare public appearance to announce his bequest, Nurmi was asked if he had competed to bring honor to Finland. His answer:

> "No. I ran for myself, never for Finland." When a reporter asked, "Not even in the Olympics?", Nurmi was even more indignant. "Not even then. Above all, not then." At the Olympics, Paavo Nurmi mattered more than ever.[51]

CHAPTER 4

Jesse Owens: Hero of the "Nazi Olympics"

Jesse Owens never forgot the first time German dictator Adolf Hitler entered Olympic Stadium in Berlin: "I remember seeing Hitler coming in with his entourage and the storm troopers standing shoulder to shoulder like an iron fence. Then came the roar of 'Heil Hitler' from one-hundred-thousand throats. And all those arms outstretched [in the Nazi salute]. It was eerie and frightening."[52]

Although Owens won four gold medals, the 1936 Summer Games are most vividly remembered as the "Nazi Olympics." Hitler, who three years later touched off fighting in World War II by invading Poland, debased the Games in an unprecedented manner. He made no secret of his intention to use the Olympics to glorify his country and his twisted theory of Aryan racial superiority. The German flag, red with the crooked black swastika that would become a symbol of evil throughout the world, rippled in the breeze alongside the five-ringed Olympic banner. German shouts of "Heil Hitler" often drowned out cheers for athletes.

Hitler, who demeaned African Americans by calling them "black auxiliaries," said, "The Americans ought to be ashamed of themselves for letting their medals be won by Negroes. I myself would never even shake hands with one of them."[53]

Owens didn't care. "It was all right with me," he said years later, a touch of satisfaction in his voice. "I didn't go to Berlin to shake hands with him, anyway. All I know is that I'm here now, and Hitler isn't."[54]

From Alabama to Cleveland

James Cleveland Owens was born September 12, 1913, in Oakville, Alabama, the grandson of former slaves and the tenth and final child of poor sharecroppers. "Not starving was the best you could do,"[55] he said of his family's bitter poverty. Henry Cleveland Owens and Emma Fitzgerald, his parents, did the best they could, but Owens admitted it was a difficult life:

My parents were not literate people—how could a share-cropper in Alabama in the first twenty years of this century get to be literate? The only thing we had was a belief in God, and we lived according to the bible. We picked cotton all day long. When I was seven, I was picking one hundred pounds a day. In the morning I'd wait in the wagon until the dew dried off. The cotton stalks were taller than me and I'd practically drown until the sun was high and the dew dried some. It was hard, and we'd sell the crop after working like demons for the summer, and then there still wasn't enough money to last the winter.[56]

Like thousands of other African Americans, the Owens family fled racism and poverty in the South by moving north to Cleveland, Ohio, in 1923. As the Owenses boarded the train to leave Alabama, Jesse's mother told him, "It's gonna take us to a better life."[57]

On his first day at Bolton Elementary School in Cleveland, Owens received a new name. When his teacher asked him his name, Owens, in the southern tradition, gave his initials. "J.C., ma'am," Owens said in a slow drawl. "Jesse?" asked the teacher, who had misunderstood. "Yes, ma'am,"[58] responded Owens, who was so nervous that he did not correct her—all he wanted to do was sit down.

A Budding Sports Star

Life was better in the North, but far from easy. Henry Owens worked in a steel mill, Emma cleaned homes, and Jesse and his siblings had part-time jobs before and after school because the family needed the money. Jesse delivered groceries and worked in a shoe repair shop, sweeping floors, washing windows, and shining shoes.

Even though Owens was often sick as a child with chronic bronchial congestion and several bouts of pneumonia that weakened his lungs, he loved running. "It was something you could do all by yourself, all under your own power," Owens said. "You could go in any direction, fast or slow, fighting the wind, seeking out new sights just on the strength of your feet and the courage of your lungs."[59]

When Owens was fourteen and began attending Fairview Junior High School, he became a star in track and basketball. At Fairview his track coach was Charles Riley, who taught Owens valuable lessons about life, gaining his love and respect. "Remember," Riley would say during workouts, "you're training for four years from next Friday, Jesse."[60] Riley made Owens realize he had to work hard *now* so he could succeed in the *future*, wise advice that helped Owens throughout his life.

In 1930 Jesse went to East Technical High School and became a nationally known track star. In June 1933 at the National Interscholastic Championship in Chicago, Owens set national high school records in the 220-yard dash and long jump and tied the high school world record for the 100-yard dash.

Those records were only a warm-up for Ohio State, which gave a scholarship to the athlete who would be called the "Buckeye Bullet."

Setting national high school records in the 220-yard dash and long jump, Jesse Owens became a nationally known track star.

The Greatest Performance in Track History

In Columbus, Ohio, Owens lived off campus with other African-American students in a boarding house because the school's lone dormitory would not accept African Americans. To earn spending money, Owens operated a freight elevator, worked in the library, and cleared tables in the school cafeteria. In the summer he worked at a gas station in Cleveland.

In 1934 Owens earned All-America honors by setting freshman records in the 100-yard and 220-yard dashes and the long jump. The next year Owens was even better, and on May 25, 1935, in the Big Ten Conference track meet in Ann Arbor, Michigan, Owens turned in the greatest one-day performance in track and field history.

In just forty-five minutes, Owens broke five world records and tied one, running 10.4 seconds in the 100-yard dash to equal that record. He leaped 26 feet, 8 1/4 inches in the long jump, a world record that stood for twenty-five years, and won the 220-yard dash in 20.3 seconds and the 200-yard low hurdles in 22.6 seconds. Owens was also credited with lowering the world records for the slightly shorter 200-meter dash and 200-meter low hurdles. Big Ten Commissioner Kenneth L. Wilson was awed: "He is a floating wonder, just like he had wings."[61]

Olympic Controversy

Owens was one of nineteen African Americans who qualified for the Olympics and would collectively win fourteen medals. Many Americans, however, did not want U.S. athletes to compete because of Hitler's racist policies toward Jews and his growing bel-

Known as "Buckeye Bullet" at Ohio State, Owens broke five world records and tied one in just forty-five minutes.

ligerence toward other nations. The German dictator had used national legislation—the so-called Nuremberg laws—to deprive Jews of their citizenship, a first step toward the Holocaust, the execution of 6 million Jews during World War II.

In 1934 Avery Brundage, a 1912 Olympian who was now president of the United States Olympic Committee (USOC), visited Germany because of concerns over Hitler's regime. Brundage came back with glowing reports about the National Socialist (Nazi) leader, and the USOC, on the basis of his recommendation, voted to attend the Olympics.

The decision was harshly criticized. In 1935 when Congress debated a resolution to boycott the games, New York Representative Emmanuel Celler claimed Brundage "prejudged the situation before he sailed from America. The rich sports commissars have snared and deluded him."[62] The Amateur Athletic Union (AAU) collected petitions signed by a half-million people seeking a boycott, and the *New York Times* opposed U.S. participation in an editorial: "When Nazis deliberately and arrogantly offend against our common humanity, sport does not transcend all political and racial considerations."[63]

USOC officials defended the decision in comments that, by today's standards, would be criticized for their insensitivity. Brundage excused what was being done by saying "the persecution of minority peoples is as old as history," adding that "the customs of other nations are not our business."

Before the Winter Games were held in Garmisch-Partenkirchen, Germany, IOC president Henri Baillet-Latour of Belgium was angered by anti-Semitic signs near Olympic facilities that declared: "Dogs and Jews not allowed." When Baillet-Latour told Hitler to have the signs removed, the Nazi dictator said, "When you are invited to a friend's house, you don't tell him how to run it, do you?" But Baillet-Latour, threatening to cancel the Olympics, responded forcefully, "When the five rings are raised over the stadium, it is no longer Germany; it is the Olympics and we are masters there."[64]

Hitler relented, but at the Summer Games the Nazis put on a show the world would not soon forget.

The Berlin Olympics

In the opening ceremonies, Austrian athletes provocatively raised their right arms in the Nazi salute and the Bulgarians entered with the stiff-legged, goose-step march favored by Hitler's elite military units. Weight lifter Rudolf Ismayr read the Olympic oath for athletes

Against Hitler's Nazi backdrop, Owens was the 1936 Olympics greatest star.

while grasping the tip of the German flag instead of the Olympic flag. When German shot-putter Hans Woelke won the first event, Hitler made a show of congratulating the gold medalist, a violation of Olympic tradition. An angry Baillet-Latour warned Hitler against such partisan displays and, after that, the dictator congratulated German winners in private.

Despite the Nazi trappings that overshadowed the Olympics, Owens was its greatest star. *The Spectator,* an English newspaper, reported that even "the German spectators, like all others, have fallen under the spell of the American Negro Jesse Owens, who is already the hero of these Games."[65] Germans cheered him with cries of "Yessa Owens, Yessa Owens," a mispronunciation due to the way Germans say the letters "J" and "W."

Owens won gold medals in the 100-meter and 200-meter dashes, the long jump, and the 400-meter relay. Like other sprinters, Owens prepared for the 100-meter race by using a trowel to scoop a hole in the track cinders for his feet, which helped him to start quickly (runners today push off from blocks to begin a race). As Owens crouched down, awaiting the starting gun, he thought about how important the race was:

> I was looking only at the finish line, and realizing that five
> of the world's fastest humans wanted to beat me to it.

There were six of us finalists, all with a gold medal ambition. Yet there could only be one winner. I thought of all the years of practice and competition, of all who had believed in me.[66]

Owens won in 10.3 seconds to tie the world record. Ralph Metcalfe, an African American who would later become an Illinois congressman, finished second. Hitler sat in stony silence during the race. He was even unhappier later, when Owens won the long jump with an assist from a German athlete.

Long jumpers had three attempts to qualify for the finals, but on his first two leaps Owens committed faults, accidental violations of the rules. "I kicked at the dirt," Owens wrote years later. "Did I come three thousand miles for this? I thought bitterly." Then Owens felt a hand on his shoulder and a voice said, "I'm Luz Long."[67] The two men began talking and Long told him, "You should be able to qualify with your eyes closed."[68]

Owens's second fault was due to stepping on the takeoff line; he should have leaped into the air before touching the line. "Jesse, let me make a suggestion," Long said. "I will place my towel a foot in front of the foul line and you can use this for your takeoff. You should then qualify easily."[69] Owens did qualify and the next day won gold with a leap of 26 feet 5 1/2 inches. Long finished second, and Hitler watched in fury as the two athletes, black and white, walked arm-in-arm in triumph. "Hitler must have gone crazy watching us embrace," said Owens.[70]

Years later Owens said he never forgot the sportsmanship displayed by Long, who was killed during World War II:

After faulting twice while qualifying for the long jump, Owens won the gold with a leap of 26 feet 5½ inches.

You can melt down all the gold medals and cups I have, and they wouldn't be plating on the twenty-four carat friendship I felt for Luz Long. I realized then, too, that Luz was the epitome of what Pierre de Coubertin must have had in mind when he said "the important thing in the Olympic Games is not winning, but taking part. The essential thing in life is not conquering but fighting well."[71]

The 200-meter dash, which Owens won in an Olympic record 20.7 seconds for his third gold medal, was to have been his last event. But in a controversial move, U.S. coaches changed the lineup of the four-man team for the 400-meter relay team, dropping Marty Glickman and Sam Stoller in favor of Owens and Metcalfe.

When Glickman and Stoller protested, Owens told the coaches, "I've won three gold medals. Let Marty and Sam have their chance."[72] But they ordered Owens to run, and the team won with a world record time of 39.8 seconds.

Many believe Glickman and Stoller, the only two U.S. Olympians who did not compete in the games, were dropped because they were Jewish. "The Germans had been terribly embarrassed by the success of our black athletes," Glickman said. "To save the Germans from further embarrassment, they didn't want to have the only two Jewish boys on the team win something, too."[73]

Even Owens admitted years later "it was the politics of our own American officials that kept them [from competing]."[74]

Owens Goes After "Real" Gold

Now one of the most famous people in the world, Owens decided to use his celebrity to make money. On August 17, the day after the Olympics ended, International News Service ran a story under his byline:

> I am turning professional because, first of all I'm busted and I know the difficulties encountered by any member of my race in getting financial security. Secondly, because if I have money, I can help my race and perhaps become like Booker T. Washington.[75]

Owens felt he had to cash in on his fame because he had a family to support. On July 5, 1935, he married Ruth Solomon, his high school sweetheart. The ceremony was actually their second wedding; three years earlier they had run away to be married just a few months before Ruth gave birth to their first child, Gloria, on August 18. Although Ruth's father had forced the couple to get an annulment in 1932, their second marriage lasted more than forty years.

Owens wins the 200-meter dash in just 20.7 seconds, an Olympic record.

Most of the moneymaking deals Owens had envisioned never materialized, and in 1936 he accepted an offer to campaign for Republican presidential candidate Alf Landon. In speeches around the nation, Owens talked about the Olympics and criticized the Democratic president, Franklin D. Roosevelt, for not meeting with him when he came back from Berlin. Roosevelt, however, easily won reelection. "It was the poorest race I ever ran, but they paid me a *lot* [more than $10,000]," Owens joked years later.[76]

Owens earned another $26,000 by late fall through a series of personal appearances at sporting events, banquets, and radio shows. He then went on a spending spree, buying a home for his young family, houses for his parents and two sisters, jewelry and clothes for Ruth, and new cars for himself and Riley, his old track coach.

Fame created some unusual moneymaking opportunities for Owens. He traveled with a comic basketball team called the Indianapolis Clowns, led a band even though he was not a musician, and raced heavyweight boxing champion Joe Louis, who won when Owens tripped. Owens admits he hated some of the things he did to make money, including running against horses. His first such race was in Cuba in December 1936:

> Of course, there's no way a man can *really* beat a horse, even over 100 yards. The secret is, get a thoroughbred because they are the most nervous animals on the planet. Then get the biggest gun you can and make sure the starter fires that big gun right by that nervous thoroughbred's ear. By the time the jockey gets the horse settled down, I could cover about 50 yards.
>
> People said it was degrading for an Olympic champion to run against a horse, but what was I supposed to do? I had four gold medals, but you can't eat four gold medals. There was no television, no big advertising, no endorsements then. Not for a black man, anyway. Things were different then.[77]

Joe Louis (heavyweight boxing champion) beat Owens in a race after he had tripped.

In the late 1930s, Owens invested thousands of dollars in a chain of dry cleaning stores that proudly proclaimed: "Speedy 7 Hour Service from The World's Fastest Runner." But the stores failed and Owens lost his money. In 1940 after his mother died, he and Ruth and their three daughters—Gloria, Beverly, and Marlene—moved to Columbus, Ohio, so he could finish his college education.

In 1951 Owens returned to Berlin for a performance with the Harlem Globetrotters basketball team; a crowd of eighty thousand people cheered him in the stadium where he had won his Olympic medals. Within a few years Owens was living in Chicago, working with youth sports programs and giving speeches to various organizations. He eventually started a public relations firm that featured one celebrity—Jesse Owens.

In *All That Glitters Is Not Gold*, William O. Johnson wrote in 1972 that "Jesse Owens is what you might call a professional good example. For this he is paid around $75,000 a year."[78] Owens was flying 250,000 miles a year to endorse a wide variety of products, make speeches, and appear at public relations events for major companies. Olympic gold was no longer the only kind he had.

A Champion Dies

In 1978 Owens and his wife moved to Scottsdale, Arizona. Although Owens had almost died in 1971 from a bout of pneumonia, he continued to smoke cigarettes and a pipe, and in 1979 the Olympic great was diagnosed with lung cancer. He died on March 31, 1980.

CHAPTER 5

Jean-Claude Killy: Racing to Glory

French skier Jean-Claude Killy once said, "I have never slowed down in my entire life and I never will. I can't do it."[79] Whether skiing to three gold medals in the 1968 Winter Olympics in Grenoble, France, driving a race car, flying a helicopter, making money in his many business ventures, or heading the effort to return the Winter Olympics to his native France, Killy has always raced through life at breakneck speed.

In fact "Casse-cou," which means "breakneck" in English, was the name French fans bestowed upon Killy, whose daring trips down treacherous, snow-clad hills resulted in broken bones as well as glorious victories. "I take all the risks," Killy once nonchalantly admitted. "That is my style. I love the feeling of danger. Skiing is my life. I cannot be afraid of it."[80]

Yet Killy's first nickname was "Toutoune," an endearing term from his father that translates as "puppy dog." And it was Killy's likable, engaging personality as well as his gold medals that made him a worldwide sports star.

In 1992 Killy gained yet another name—copresident of Le Comité d'Organization des Jeux Olympiques—as he helped preside over the 1992 Winter Olympics in Albertville, France. Killy by age forty-eight had matured, maybe even slowed down just a bit, and fully realized the magnitude of his new role. When asked to compare his two Olympic experiences, Killy answered:

Jean-Claude Killy (right) is the only gold medalist to become a member of the IOC and in 1999 was being considered as a future IOC president.

When I was a skier in Grenoble in 1968, I was the only one at stake. I alone would have suffered the consequences of a fall. In 1992, in Albertville, what is at stake far exceeds the purely sporting aspect, and the consequences of organizing the Games affect much more than myself alone. So, you will easily understand the pressure is far greater in 1992 than it was in 1968. Perhaps, though, it is only a question of age.[81]

Young Killy Takes to the Slopes

Killy was born August 30, 1943, in the Paris suburb of St. Cloud. During World War II his father, Robert Killy, was a pilot for French forces that continued to fight after Germany took control of France. When the war ended in 1945, Killy moved his family to Val-d'Isère, a small, remote village in the Savoie region of the French Alps.

Val-d'Isère today is a world-famous ski resort. But when Killy, his wife, Madeleine, and two young children—two-year-old Jean-Claude and his four-year-old sister France—arrived, it was only beginning to be known for its magnificent skiing. As Val-d'Isère prospered, so did Killy, an excellent skier who took advantage of his expertise to open a ski rental business. Killy was so successful that he also built a small hotel and restaurant.

When Jean-Claude came to Val-d'Isère he had a frail constitution, but the clear mountain air strengthened him and by age three he had found the great passion of his life—skiing. He loved racing down the slopes surrounding Val-d'Isère and was soon skiing faster than anyone his age. "I can't remember when I wasn't a skier," Killy has written. "I remember traveling by bus to race at Thollon-les-Memises when I was only seven or eight, and thinking how privileged I was to get to travel."[82]

When Jean-Claude was six years old, his mother abandoned the family for another man and the Killys divorced. Jean-Claude and his younger brother, Michel, remained with their father while France lived with grandparents. The divorce changed young Jean-Claude's life dramatically, shaping his personality. Although it seems strange for someone who is so famous, Killy became shy. At the 1968 Olympics he said:

I am incredibly shy. I know that it is ridiculous that I should still be so shy, but when I am away from the French ski team, my gang, I just don't open my mouth. It's terribly difficult for me to be with people I don't know. This shyness has made me push harder in my skiing.[83]

Killy had to care for his younger brother. "I was responsible for a lot of things at home for as long as I can remember," Killy said. "Maybe that's why I always felt older than other kids my age."[84] He also became very close to his father. "My attitudes toward life were formed entirely under my father's influence," Killy has said.[85]

Robert Killy was so busy with his new businesses that he sent his sons to boarding schools in the valley miles below the mountain village. While attending school in Chambery some eighty miles away, the eleven-year-old Killy was stricken with tuberculosis and spent several months recuperating in a sanitarium.

As a teenager, Killy pursued skiing with a passion. Whether back home in Val-d'Isère or anywhere else that had a snow-covered hill, he was nearly always on skis, even skipping class to ski. After attending four different secondary schools Killy, an indifferent student, quit at age sixteen to pursue his great love. He left with the blessing of his father. "When Jean-Claude was nine, ten, he was faster than the best instructor at Val-d'Isère," Killy said. "At sixteen he had to leave school. I decided, I decided for him, because he was very good."[86]

At the time it was common in Europe for young skiers to pursue their sport full-time, but Killy's lack of formal education has always bothered him. Even though his English was good, at the 1968 Olympics Killy apologized to a reporter for his lack of schooling, which he felt limited how he expressed himself. But through the years Killy would acquire a polished elegance and mastery of business that helped him become a success even though he lacked a university education.

Budding Superstar

When Killy first became a member of the French ski team in 1960, he was so reckless in his quest for victory that he never finished a race; he would ski too fast and fall, whether it was in a downhill, slalom, or giant slalom race. The three races in Alpine skiing all have one constant—speed. The downhill is the most daring and dangerous, with speed the only requirement as skiers plummet like bullets down a steep trail that is nearly two miles long and has at least an eight-hundred-meter vertical drop. Skiers approach speeds of eighty miles an hour, going airborne after hitting small bumps as they rocket down the course in less than two minutes.

Speed is also essential in slalom, but in this event skiers have to maneuver tightly through between fifty-five and seventy-five "gates" that wind down the course in serpentine fashion. The gates are formed by lightweight poles stuck in the snow, and a skier is disqualified for missing a gate. Giant slalom, also called "super-G," is a hybrid of downhill and slalom. Because it has fewer gates than slalom, racers ski the course in long, sweeping turns that allow them to go faster, as in downhill, but they can still be disqualified for missing a gate.

Killy's daring in challenging the slippery ski slopes with every ounce of speed he could muster excited fans. But French coach Honoré Bonnet said it was not a smart way to compete:

> He'd be ahead by two seconds halfway down, but he'd fall. I encouraged him. I told him that I selected people not by their finish but by their performance in the gates on the way down. I reminded him that, of course, if he wanted ever to win, he would have to arrange to also finish.[87]

Killy as a youth had broken leg and ankle bones in high-speed spills. He still suffered some injuries as a result of his recklessness before finally learning how to ski under control. He won his first international race in January 1961, a slalom event, and three years later was good enough to ski, but not win, in the 1964 Winter Olympics in Innsbruck, Austria.

"Technically, I think I was skiing well enough to have won some medals there, but I didn't have a winning attitude," Killy admits. "I was careless in preparing my equipment. I was strong enough physically, but I was too impressed by other racers. Consequently, I lacked the confidence necessary to ski aggressively."[88]

The Rich Life of "Amateur" Skiing

Between 1964 and 1968, except for a mandatory two-year stint in the French army, in which he served in Algeria, Killy lived the fast-paced life of an "amateur," traveling the world to race. But Killy and other skiers were amateurs in name only. Skiing had become big business, and equipment manufacturers began paying top performers to endorse their products. The payments were allegedly secret, even though the ski world and Olympic officials knew in general what was going on.

In *Comeback*, Killy talks openly about money he made as an amateur:

> There's no way we racers could have lived the lives we did without money. We were totally dedicated to skiing, working twenty-four hours a day at it all year round. In the summer, we traveled to the Southern Hemisphere for ski testing and additional training. All this took money. We had money from the French Ski Federation, from the Ministry of Sport, and from the pool of equipment manufacturers.

That was official. But in addition we were getting paid as individuals. Everyone was getting paid—except maybe the Americans, and some of them, for sure, had their deals, too. From my various sources I made about $40,000 in 1967 and again in 1968.[89]

The more races a skier won, the more he was paid, and Killy's price tag shot up in 1965 after he won the slalom at the Hahnenkamm, a premier event in Austria. "That was the breakthrough I needed to ski aggressively in every race," Killy said. "You can't ski at maximum speed unless you're psychologically prepared—confident of your ability and know you can win."[90] His first downhill victory in international competition was a race in Chile in the 1966–1967 ski season, a year in which he won twelve of sixteen events to become the world's top skier.

The secret payments escalated and Killy accepted them, even though he knew they were wrong:

In 1968, Killy won all three Alpine ski events in his native France to become a national hero and best-known sports figure.

I was clearly in violation of Olympic rules and so were many other major competitors. We thought that Avery Brundage and the International Olympic Committee [IOC] were probably aware of what was going on, but, of course, we didn't want to challenge them directly. It seemed perfectly natural that we should make money to put aside for our non-racing days. We would not have skied if it had been otherwise. I don't say what we were doing was right. The whole system was wrong, and the hypocrisy extended up to the highest levels.[91]

Olympic Glory and Commercialism

In 1956 Toni Sailer of Austria became the first Olympian to win all three Alpine ski events. In 1968 Killy duplicated the feat in his native France to become a national hero and one of the world's best-known sports figures.

The first race was the downhill, and Killy crossed the finish line in 1:59.85, just 0.08 second faster than France's Guy Perillat. The victory was all the more remarkable because during a practice run, Killy had skied across a patch of ice, stripping the wax from the bottom of his skis. He had no time to apply more wax, but won even though wax enables skiers to race faster. "Winning the downhill gave me confidence and took some of the pressure off,"[92] he admits.

The end of the race featured an incident that highlighted the growing debate over amateurism. In Grenoble, Olympic officials

Even though the wax from the bottom of his skis had been stripped off during a practice run, Killy was able to cross the finish line first in the men's downhill.

took skis away from competitors before they were photographed. This move was designed to prevent the successful athletes from publicizing the brands of their skis.

Killy, who was paid to use Dynamic skis, circumvented that by having a friend, Michel Arpin, rush out to embrace him while wearing a pouch that prominently displayed the word "Dynamic." Arpin also took one of his own skis, which had Dynamic's recognizable trademark of two yellow bars, and planted it in the snow beside Killy's head. This ensured Dynamic would receive free advertising when Killy was photographed.

Killy won the slalom in 1:39.73 seconds and the giant slalom in 3:29.28. Thanks to foggy conditions the morning of the race, it was the slalom race that provided the most excitement.

In the slalom, skiers race the course twice. At first it appeared that Haaken Mjoen of Norway had beaten Killy, but he was disqualified for missing gates. Then Karl Schranz of Austria won approval for a third run after claiming he had had to ski around some gates to avoid a person who had wandered onto the fog-shrouded course. After his third run, the Austrian appeared to have beaten Killy. But after a long argument, officials ruled that Schranz missed two gates on his original second run, before the unknown person had appeared on the course, and he was also disqualified.

Although Killy rejoiced in his Olympic triple triumph, years later he admitted time had put his accomplishment into perspective: "I thought I would be a superman. But nothing happened at all. I was exactly the same as before. I learned that success is like a big ghost. You catch it and there is nothing there."[93]

Cashing In on Olympic Gold

Killy retired from competitive skiing, asking rhetorically, "What can I expect more than an Olympic gold medal? It's the climax of my career and that's the end of it."[94]

But it was only the beginning of a new life that consisted, at first, of cashing in on his Olympic fame. His movie star good looks and debonair manner made him an ideal spokesperson, and sports agent Mark McCormack helped Killy sign six-figure contracts with more than a hundred companies that manufactured everything from automobiles to watches and skis.

The Olympic champion also performed in television specials and starred in a movie, *Snow Job,* which even he admitted was awful. But Killy had acted in the movie to be with his fiancée, actress Daniele Gaubert, who he met in Val-d'Isère. Although Killy

After retiring from competitive skiing, Killy worked as a spokesperson, performed in television specials, and even starred in a movie.

had a reputation as a playboy, he said it was undeserved. "Most of that was media ballyhoo," he said. "I don't claim to be made of wood, but I'm not an aspiring Casanova, either."[95]

He was faithful to Gaubert from their first meeting, wedding her in 1973 and staying happily married until she died of cancer in 1987. They had one daughter, Emilie, and Killy adopted two of his wife's children from a previous marriage.

Killy returned to racing in the 1972–1974 season on the professional International Ski Racers Association, winning a tour-leading $68,625. But Killy then began to concentrate on business, establishing a successful ski-wear company, endorsing products, and engaging in other ventures, all of which by 1990 had earned him a fortune estimated at $20 million.

Back to the Olympics

In 1986 Killy was named copresident of the Albertville organizing committee with Michel Barnier, president of the Savoie General Council, a regional legislature. Returning the Olympics to France was a job that consumed Killy's life, especially after the death of his wife. He traveled the world, first to convince IOC delegates to award the Olympics to Albertville and then to organize the Winter Games, including raising an estimated $850 million to finance them.

It was a difficult task even for Killy, who was used to handling large sums of money in business. "We had to find close to one-billion dollars, and then spend it. I know business well, but all of this was two zeros larger than I was accustomed to,"[96] he said.

The huge success of the 1992 Olympics was seen as the skier's personal triumph. It was a claim he adamantly denied. "This is not the power of Jean-Claude Killy," he said shortly before the Winter Games. "It is the power of the five [Olympic] rings."[97]

From Hero to Elder Statesman

Perhaps the most surprising thing about Killy is that the daring young speedster who dominated the 1968 Winter Games has matured into an elder statesman of the Olympic movement. The only gold medalist to serve as the head of a future Olympics, Killy became a member of the IOC in 1992 and by 1999 was being touted as a future IOC president.

Despite problems they have had over the years, Killy reveres the Olympics for many of the same reasons Baron Pierre de Coubertin did. "There is truth here and there [to criticisms]," Killy admits, "but in Olympic solidarity, in the five rings, there are a lot more pluses than negatives."[98]

CHAPTER 6

Mark Spitz: Olympic Glory Dimmed by Olympic Tragedy

For swimmer Mark Spitz, the news conference September 5, 1972, should have been one of the most joyous experiences in his life. The day before in Munich, Germany, Spitz had won his seventh gold medal in the 400-meter medley relay team race. Having won more gold medals than any athlete in a single Olympics, Spitz could now bask in the spotlight of the world's media and brag about his historic accomplishment, two things he dearly loved to do.

Instead, the media session became one of the most terrifying moments of his life.

A smiling Spitz arrived at 9 A.M., only to learn that Arab terrorists just hours earlier had killed two Israeli athletes and taken hostage nine other Israeli Olympians. He became frightened that terrorists might attack him because he was Jewish. "I don't want to get up at that microphone," Spitz said. "I'd be a perfect target for someone with a gun."[99]

Instead of standing tall at the podium, happily smiling and answering questions, Spitz remained seated, hiding behind a protective shield formed by three American swimming coaches. Reporters could barely see Spitz and had trouble hearing his answers. The disjointed news conference quickly fell apart and Spitz told a coach, "Let's get the hell out of here."[100]

Mark Spitz (center) at a news conference in Munich, where hours earlier, Arab terrorists had stormed the Olympic Village.

A few hours later Spitz left the country on the recommendation of German officials, who shared his concern he might be in danger. Spitz flew to England from Furstenfeldbruck, the airport where nine Israeli hostages would be killed the next day, as the terrorist attack came to a violent, tragic end.

Spitz Learns to Swim—and Win

Born February 10, 1950, in Modesto, California, Mark Andrew Spitz and his family moved to Hawaii when he was a youngster. It was there that Arnold Spitz taught his young son to swim:

> I learned to swim when I was about six years old. [My father] taught me to swim underwater first, because he felt—and I share the feeling—that the fear of water comes from the desire to stay on top of the water while the natural tendency of the body is to go under. The whole idea of swimming is that you are trying to manipulate yourself in a different environment and so the way to start out properly is to get acquainted with that different environment, to make friends with the water.[101]

By the time Spitz was eight years old, his family was living in Sacramento, California, and he was winning races at a local YMCA. When Spitz was nine, he began swimming for Sherman Chavoor, coach of the Arden Hills Swim and Tennis Club.

Although Spitz would later work with several other coaches including James "Doc" Counsilman at Indiana University, Chavoor was his favorite. When Spitz was in college he returned home each summer to work with Chavoor, who in 1972 was an Olympic coach. Chavoor said Spitz became a great swimmer because he dedicated himself to training hard. "This guy," Chavoor said in Munich, "has worked every day, three-four-five hours for twelve-thirteen years. He would like to surpass any other swimmer."[102]

When Spitz was ten, he set his first national age group record by swimming the 50-yard butterfly in 50 seconds flat. It was the first of more than thirty-five records Spitz would set in the next twelve years, including ten in the year leading up to the 1972 Olympics.

The butterfly became Spitz's specialty. "The first time I ever won a national championship," Spitz recalls, "I was sixteen years old in Lincoln, Nebraska. I won the 100-meter butterfly and my time was 58.2 seconds. The world record at that time was 57 seconds flat. I broke the record the next year when I was seventeen with a time of 56.3 seconds."[103]

The butterfly is the most difficult stroke in swimming, demanding both technically and physically. As such it was perfect for Spitz, who was willing to spend more time in the water than other swimmers to refine technique and build strength and stamina. Most swimmers excel in only one or two events, but Spitz trained so hard that he was able to set world records at various distances and with different strokes. Spitz believes his versatility came from his early years of swimming:

> I was trained as a distance swimmer when I was young, and that enabled me at a later date to be a sprinter, since I had been conditioned for the long haul—for endurance. In sprints, it's the swimmer who can hold out the longest—at a higher rate of speed—who wins. And it is much easier, I feel, to go from distance to sprints than it is to go from sprints to distance [events].[104]

Becoming the Best in the World

When Spitz was fourteen he began swimming for the well-known Santa Clara Swim Club coached by George Haines. Spitz would get up every morning at 5 A.M. and his mother, Lenore, would make the long drive there for workouts. His family eventually moved to make it easier for him to train.

Spitz had trouble getting along with older Santa Clara stars like Don Schollander, who in 1964 had won four gold medals in Tokyo, Japan. Part of Spitz's problem was the sense of supreme confidence his father had instilled in him, which made him seem arrogant. Arnold Spitz contributed to his son's negative image with comments like the one he made after his fifteen-year-old son won four races in his international debut at the World Maccabean Games in Israel:

> I've got my life tied up in this kid. He's beautiful. He's exceptional. If people don't like it, the hell with them. Swimming isn't everything, *winning* is. I told him I didn't care about winning age groups, I care about [breaking] world records.[105]

Because Spitz felt rejected by Santa Clara swimmers, he ignored them, concentrating instead on proving how good he was. "I learned head games from Schollander," said Spitz. "I learned to walk the pool deck with an arrogant aura."[106] The result was that Spitz would never be very popular with his teammates, even when he was winning medal after medal in Munich.

When Spitz was older he grew a mustache, which also set him apart from his teammates. Swimmers usually cut their hair short and many even shave their heads and bodies, hoping to be able to swim faster by making their bodies more aerodynamic. Spitz says he wore the mustache because "it looks pretty good on me" and

At eighteen years old, Spitz swam in his first Olympics in Mexico City, where he brought home four medals.

claims it "helps my swimming. It catches the water and keeps it out of my mouth."[107] Other swimmers believed the mustache symbolized his vanity and that he wore it so fans could easily recognize him.

In 1968 Spitz swam in his first Olympics in Mexico City, Mexico. The eighteen-year-old won gold medals in the four-by-100-meter and four-by-200-meter freestyle relays (a relay is a race in which four swimmers compete as a team), silver in the 100-meter butterfly, and bronze in the 100-meter freestyle. Despite winning four medals, it proved to be an embarrassing showing because Spitz had foolishly predicted he would win six gold medals.

After his humbling Olympic debut, Spitz enrolled in Indiana University and competed for four years under Doc Counsilman, who is considered the greatest swimming coach in collegiate history. Spitz dedicated himself to improving, and by the 1972 Olympics he had set twenty-six world records, won five gold medals at the 1967 Pan American Games, captured eight National Collegiate Athletic Association titles, and received the 1971 Sullivan Award as the nation's top amateur athlete.

Although Spitz did not make any predictions—he had learned from his mistake four years earlier—the news media claimed he could win seven gold medals. "It's tremendous, the pressure of not losing," Spitz said of the high expectations. "It's reached a point where my self-esteem comes into it. I just don't want to lose."[108]

Seven Golds, Seven World Records

In eight days in Munich, Spitz lived up to the nickname given him by a German newspaper, "Mark der Hai (the shark)," by winning gold medals and setting world records in every event he entered: three individual and four relay races.

His first race August 28 was the 200-meter butterfly. It had been his final event in Mexico City and he had finished last, which made the 6-foot, 170-pound Spitz nervous before the race. When he won, Spitz leaped out of the water, his arms held high in victory: He had not only finished first and set a world record (2:00.70), he had shattered the psychological specter of failure that had haunted him for four years.

Later that night Spitz helped the United States capture gold in the four-by-100-meter freestyle (3:26.42), and the next day he overtook teammate Steve Genter on the last lap to win the 200-meter freestyle (1:52.78). His fourth and fifth gold medals came three days later when he captured the 100-meter butterfly (54.27) and anchored the four-by-200-meter freestyle relay team (7:35.78).

Because Spitz had already surpassed Schollander's 1968 performance, Spitz considered dropping out of the 100-meter freestyle to save his energy for the four-by-100-meter medley relay. But coach Chavoor warned Spitz he had to swim the race: "Listen Mark, if you don't swim the hundred meters, you might as well go home now. They'll say you're 'Chicken, that you're afraid to face [U.S. teammate] Jerry Heidenreich.'"[109]

After the 1968 Olympics, Spitz enrolled in Indiana University and competed under coach Doc Counsilman and by the 1972 Olympics, he had set twenty-six world records.

On September 3, Spitz won the 100 meters in 51.22, beating Heidenreich by nearly a half-second. The next day Spitz took his historic seventh gold medal in the four-by-100-meter medley relay and helped set another world record of 3:26.42.

Although one U.S. swimmer sarcastically remarked that "it could have happened to a nicer guy," after the race teammates lifted Spitz to their shoulders and carried him on a victory lap around the pool. Spitz framed the photo and said years later, "I enjoy [that picture] more than the one that was taken with the seven gold medals around my neck. Having a tribute from your teammates is a feeling that can never be duplicated."[110]

Terror in Munich

But within hours of the most golden moment in Mark Spitz's life, terror descended on the Summer Games. At 4:30 A.M. September 5, a band of eight members of a terrorist group calling themselves Black September scaled fences surrounding the Olympic Village and battered their way into rooms housing the Israeli weight-lifting team, killing two of the athletes. The terrorists then took nine Israelis hostage, demanding the release of some two hundred Arab prisoners held in Israel and other countries for guerilla activities.

Members of Black September were motivated by the enmity that had existed between Jews and Moslems for centuries. In 1948

Motivated by the enmity that existed between Jews and Moslems, Arab terrorists stormed the Olympic Village in Munich, killing two athletes and kidnapping nine.

when the nation of Israel was established for the Jewish people, the ancient quarrel exploded anew, and neighboring Arab states vowed to overthrow Israel and take back land they believed rightfully belonged to Palestinian Arabs. The disagreement resulted in border clashes and terrorist attacks that have continued throughout the twentieth century.

People around the world watched the tense situation unfold live on television. When the terrorists demanded to be flown out of Germany, they were taken with their hostages to the Munich airport early on September 6. Before they could board the plane, German police opened fire, and in the ensuing battle nine Israeli athletes, five Arabs, and one policeman were killed. Most of the Israelis died when one of the terrorists detonated a hand grenade. The three surviving terrorists were arrested.

The world reacted in horror to the massacre, and requests poured in to halt the Olympics. "Enough blood has flowed to end the Games,"[111] said Joseph Inbar, president of the Israeli Olympic Committee. But International Olympic Commission president Avery Brundage announced that the Games would continue:

The coffins of the eleven Israeli Olympians killed by the Arab terrorists arrive in Tel Aviv.

Every civilized person recoils in horror at the barbarous criminal intrusion of terrorists into peaceful Olympic precincts. We mourn our Israeli friends, victims of this brutal assault. We have only the strength of a great ideal. I am sure the public will agree that we cannot allow a handful of terrorists to destroy this nucleus of international cooperation and goodwill we have in the Olympic movement.[112]

Brundage was criticized for allowing the Olympics to continue, but many athletes thought it was the right decision. Said Soviet long-jumper Igor Tervanesian: "It is terrible what happened. I don't feel like competing now. But it is good the Games continue. Terrorists should not be able to disrupt the Olympics."[113]

Post-Olympic Gold

Spitz retired after the 1972 Olympics to cash in on his fame, a tradition that had begun with U.S. swimmer Johnny Weissmuller, who parlayed five gold medals in 1924 and 1928 into a movie career as Tarzan. A photograph of Spitz, seven gold medals dangling from his neck, sold 300,000 copies. It became the second-best-selling poster in history, trailing only the swimsuit pose of leggy movie star Betty Grable, World War II's most popular pinup.

Scrapping his plan to become a dentist, Spitz pursued every commercial opportunity available and made $5 million in endorsements the first year after Munich. Asked how many offers he had, Spitz joked,

> How many clouds are in the sky? I'm a commodity, an endorser. It's like a game to see how much money I can make. It's just amazing to me. I thought maybe I'd make enough to pay my way through dental school. But I guess I've caught on as a symbol or something. I know I'm lucky, but I also feel I am entitled to make a buck.[114]

In 1973 Spitz married model Suzy Weiner (they appeared that week on the cover of *Sports Illustrated*) and they had two sons, Mark and Justin. Spitz lived the comfortable life of a successful California businessman, starting a swimwear and athletic clothing business, endorsing products, and engaging in other business enterprises.

But in 1989, Spitz decided he needed another challenge: he began training for the 1992 Olympics in Barcelona, Spain.

The Martian Man

It was unheard of for someone to take seventeen years off from competition and make a comeback at the advanced age of thirty-nine. But Spitz, who had not lost any of the confidence or arrogance that helped propel him to seven gold medals, predicted in a 1990 *Time* magazine interview he would make the U.S. team:

> All bets are off. I am the Martian man come to life in sports. If you had to create a situation to test the body, here's a guy who was great. He has taken care of himself. He has been sort of hibernating, time warped. We'll see what happens. I think we're going to redefine what forty-year-olds can do.[115]

Spitz (far right) decided to train for the 1992 Olympics at the age of thirty-nine, but after taking seventeen years off, he was unable to swim fast enough.

In the end, the comeback fizzled: Spitz simply could not swim fast enough to make the team. But he did capture something the cocky young gold medalist of his youth never had—the respect and goodwill of many of his former critics, as the public and younger athletes he swam against embraced his nostalgic return to the water.

"By making a comeback," Spitz said, "I'm changing the attitude of people toward me. If I'd known that people would react so enthusiastically, I'd have done it years ago. Everyone loves to be loved."[116]

And Spitz *finally* felt loved.

CHAPTER 7

Vasily Alexeyev:
The Soviet Hercules

People of every nation in every period of history have revered strength. Their admiration, adulation, and sheer awe of the most powerful men who walked among them is embedded in the mythology of various cultures: the biblical Samson, who lost his strength when Delilah cut his hair, regained it when his hair grew back, and toppled huge stone pillars to bring a temple crashing down upon his enemies; Hercules, so strong as an infant that he strangled huge snakes sent to kill him; and Atlas, the Greek god who supported the world on his shoulders.

In *The Big Red Machine*, Yuri Brokhin states that Russians, too, have always prized their strongest men:

> There has always been a cult of physical strength in Russia. The earliest folk heroes were lauded most for restraining wild horses, bending copper coins, and straightening iron horseshoes with their bare hands. In later centuries, crowds at carnivals fell into ecstasy when strong men single-handedly lifted wagons or a horse's collar with five men hanging on. In the [1970s and 1980s] the superheavyweight lifter has become a Russian trademark. His muscles drawing more respect from the average man than the most spectacular Sputnik [Russian satellite] stuffed with every miracle of modern electronics.[117]

The superheavyweight class for weight lifters tipping the scale at more than 250 pounds made its first appearance at the 1972 Olympics in Munich, Germany. So did Vasily Alexeyev, who won the first of his two consecutive gold medals.

Alexeyev was a giant of a man who carried well over 300 pounds of fat and muscle on his 6 feet, 1 1/2-inch frame. For nearly a decade, no one in the world was stronger. Alexeyev was undefeated in competition from 1970 to 1978, set eighty world records, and was known as the Russian Hercules.

Vasily Alexeyev was undefeated in competition from 1970 to 1978, setting eighty world records.

Lyn Jones, coaching director for the United States Olympic team, believes Alexeyev was the greatest weight lifter of all time and one of the greatest Olympic champions in any sport. "He broke more world records than any other athlete in any sport in the history of the world. He is an absolute icon in Olympic sport," says Jones.[118]

From Lumberjack to Russian Hero

Alexeyev was born in 1942 in Pokrov, a small community in the northern part of Russia, which at that time was part of the Union of Soviet Socialist Republics. His father was a lumberjack, and as a young man Alexeyev worked in a timber camp, where he gained the respect of other lumberjacks for his ability to lift massive logs. His first set of barbells is said to have been the wheels and axle of a timber truck.

Although Alexeyev became a mining engineer, he continued lifting weights and in 1966 began training formally in Shakhty, a coal-mining city about eight hundred miles southwest of Moscow. At the age of twenty-four, Alexeyev was old to start competing in a new sport, but it was not long before the world began learning of his prowess.

Only three years later Alexeyev finished third in the Soviet championship, a solid showing. But Alexeyev scrawled "I want to be first" across a photograph of the top finishers and boasted to sports officials, "Next year I'm going to *press* the weight Toad snatched today."[119] "Toad" was the nickname of Leonid Zhabotinsky (the Russian word for toad is *zhaba*), the heavyweight gold medalist in 1964 and 1968.

Zhabotinsky had snatched 210 kilograms (a kilogram is 2.2 pounds), and in January 1970 Alexeyev pressed a world record 219.5 kilograms (595 pounds) and he won the Soviet title. Alexeyev's fulfillment of his vow was amazing because it is more difficult to press weight than to snatch it.

For Alexeyev, the horn that signaled a successful lift quickly became a familiar sound of victory.

Types of Lift

To appreciate Alexeyev's achievement, one must understand the types of lift. When Alexeyev won his first gold medal, competitors performed three lifts: the *press,* the *snatch,* and the *clean and jerk.* In the press, the lifter pulled the weighted bar to chest level and extended it overhead using *only* his arms. This press was eliminated after 1972 because officials had trouble judging the legality of some lifts; competitors started employing barely discernible body shifts and jolts to allow their more powerful leg and trunk muscles to help them move the weight.

The snatch, the more technical and explosive of the two lifts still used, is performed in one continuous movement. The lifter pulls the bar to about chest height and then, in the moment before the bar starts to descend, pulls his body into a squat position under the bar, which he secures overhead with arms held straight. The lifter must then stand and wait for the referees' "down" signal, which is usually indicated by the sounding of a horn.

More weight can be lifted in the clean and jerk. In the "clean" part of the lift, the bar is pulled to about waist level and before the bar starts to descend, the lifter pulls his body beneath the bar, secures the bar on his shoulders or chest, and stands erect. In the "jerk" that follows, the lifter thrusts the bar overhead in one motion, splits his legs front and back, and brings his feet together. The lifter again must await the down signal before lowering the bar.

In both lifts, the down signal is not given until the lifter is motionless. The winner is the one who has scored the highest total number of pounds in all the lifts: three through 1972 and just two after that.

1972 Gold Medalist

In 1970 the unknown Alexeyev exploded onto the weight-lifting scene, quickly becoming known as the world's strongest man by winning the first of eight straight Soviet and world championships. That year he also became the first to lift 500 pounds and to total more than 600 kilograms (1,323 pounds) in the three competive lifts.

Because Olympic competition is computed in metric figures, the lift of 500 pounds (about 227 kilograms) at a competition in Columbus, Ohio, in October 1970 did not seem significant to Alexeyev; it was just an odd number of kilograms to him, even though it awed Americans. But Alexeyev knew cracking the 600-kilo barrier was special. When he did it, a Russian newspaper ran this huge headline in capital letters on its front page:

MARCH 19, 1970: A NEW ERA IN WEIGHT-LIFTING HISTORY BEGAN TODAY: THE COSMIC BARRIER OF 600 HAS BEEN BROKEN BY A SOVIET ATHLETE.[120]

Alexeyev began breaking so many records that he made Soviet officials nervous; the reason was that the government gave athletes the equivalent of $1,500 for every world record they set.

Alexeyev attempts to lift 240 kg doing the "clean and jerk" lift.

After Alexeyev had shattered seven world records in one day—June 27, 1971, in a national meet in Moscow—the government reduced the rewards to $700 and counted only records set in international competition.

But world championships and world records were only a prelude to Munich, when Alexeyev set Olympic records in all four categories of the competition: the clean and jerk (230 kilograms/507.1 pounds), the press (235 kilograms/518.1 pounds), the snatch (175 kilograms/385.8 pounds), and the three-lift total (640 kilograms/1,410.9 pounds).

Lyn Jones, who was coach of the Australian team in 1972, says that Alexeyev revolutionized weight lifting by being the first big man to concentrate on technique. "They used to achieve their success more by brute force," Jones says, "but after Alexeyev came through with his beautiful technique, which he had despite his very large belly, it was necessary for big men to be technically correct as well as just strong."[121]

Jones also believes Alexeyev won partly by intimidating his opponents:

> The guy had a presence which you had to see in person to understand. When he walked into the training hall, everybody stopped. It was like, "Here's Vasily." And when he showed up for competitions, he had such a dominating effect on people. It was just the presence of this huge man. Nobody could beat him.[122]

Soviet Sports Hero

For Alexeyev, Olympic gold was a passport to a rich new life as a certified sports hero in the Soviet Union. As part of its propaganda war against the United States and other democratically governed nations, the Soviet Union tried to prove the superiority of its communist system by dominating in the Olympics and other sporting events. Alexeyev became the biggest, most recognizable star in a Soviet sports bureaucracy that became known as the Big Red Machine.

In the 1970s, the Soviet Union listed Alexeyev's occupation as mining engineer and his salary was 500 rubles (about $700) a month, relatively high for the Soviet Union. Yet he never worked as an engineer, and the cost of his lifestyle far exceeded his stated salary. In a gross understatement that was tinged with the playful boasting he was known for, Alexeyev explained why he did not work steadily at his presumed occupation:

Shattering seven world records at a national meet in Moscow was only a prelude to Alexeyev's success in Munich, where he set Olympic records in all four categories of competition.

Becoming famous as I have been is not all positive. It makes it more difficult to go forward in your working career. Of course, I am not striving to go upward in my career at this moment. If I achieve too much as a mining engineer, it becomes more difficult to pursue my training as a sportsman. I also know that if I were working my way up in my mining engineer career, I would be a big chief by now.[123]

While most families lived in small apartments, Alexeyev, his wife Olimpiada, and their sons Sergei and Dmitri, had a small estate to themselves, a spacious home in Shakhty that was surrounded by a high brick wall for privacy. He rented the home from the government for only 12 rubles (about $17) a month. Alexeyev also had a car worth $10,000, a luxury that for most Soviet citizens was only a dream.

In 1975 *Sports Illustrated* writer William O. Johnson visited Alexeyev in Shakhty. It was rare then for American journalists to travel in the Soviet Union, and Johnson came away with unique insights into Soviet sports and the world's strongest man. Leonid Tkach, a high-ranking sports official, told Johnson the town's sports committee saw to all of Alexeyev's needs:

> The point of our [sports] system is to treat them well. The better sportsmen get better living conditions, better working conditions. If a sportsman produces better results in sports, then he gets better food, better house, better job perhaps. Certainly a great sportsman like Vasily Alexeyev must live better than anyone else.[124]

The special privileges the Soviet Union gave its athletes allowed them to live in comfort and train full time instead of working at a day job, advantages that other countries claimed gave them an unfair advantage and made them professional athletes instead of amateurs.

Johnson discovered that Alexeyev, far from the menacing figure he seemed to be during competition, had a pleasant, almost whimsical personality. Alexeyev enjoyed listening and singing along to records by English rock star Tom Jones, was a warm-hearted, loving father, and enjoyed tending his prized tomatoes and Bulgarian peppers. "Ahhh," Alexeyev sighed while showing off his beloved garden, "to make something in the earth, that is the best recreation yet. I have made many things in this earth."[125]

Alexeyev was boastful in a playful way. "It is a fact," Alexeyev said, "that I have the best singing voice on the Soviet weightlifting team. When I was a boy in the north of Russia I was a musician and I sang at weddings. I was very popular."[126] Alexeyev also claimed to be the best on his team at table tennis, dominos, billiards, and even cooking, which he proved by making lunch for Johnson.

Gold Again in 1976

At the 1976 Olympics in Montreal, Alexeyev broke his Olympic record in the snatch (185 kilograms/407.9 pounds), set a new world record in the clean and jerk (255 kilograms/562.2 pounds), and won the gold medal for his two-lift total (440 kilograms/970.1 pounds).

His second gold was not supposed to have been as easy because he was facing a stiff challenge from twenty-four-year-old Gerd Bonk of East Germany, who in April had beaten him for the European championship. But just before the Olympic showdown began, Alexeyev said in a loud voice that rolled like thunder, "Bonk could not even beat me if I were fifty years old."[127]

In Montreal, Canada, each of the eleven superheavyweights had three attempts at both the snatch and the clean and jerk. While the other ten lifted lower weights, Alexeyev ignored them by staying in a training room. When Bonk quit after lifting 170 kilograms (374 pounds) in the snatch, Alexeyev came out and on his first attempt raised 175 kilograms (385.5 pounds), his 1972 Olympic record. He then heaved up 185 kilograms (408 pounds) to break that mark.

The clean and jerk was Alexeyev's best event and again, the Soviet champion did not come out until Bonk had lifted 235 kilos (518 pounds) on his last attempt. Alexeyev asked that the bar be loaded with 255 kilograms (562 pounds) and then lifted it to set another world record and win the gold. This is how Yuri Brokhin describes the incredible lift:

> He adjusts the leather support belt beneath his royal belly and drops his hands relaxedly to his sides. His muscles flow soft and elastic along his arms, unlike the useless bulge and definition characteristic of body-builders. He snatches the huge weight in a single, even, organic motion, raising the barbell over his head as if it were a woolen sweater. Alexeyev waddles off the platform like any Russian [worker] after a day's work well done—he might as easily have been felling trees, mining coal, or laying bricks. Today he happens to be lifting weights, but tomorrow, if asked nicely, he'll be eager to tow an ailing tractor.[128]

Alexeyev was smugly satisfied to have won again despite predictions he would not repeat as champion. "I am pleased to be the strongest man in the world for my two children, my two boys. Maybe now my wife will show more respect,"[129] he joked to reporters.

A Giant Grows Old

When Alexeyev won his second gold medal he was thirty-four years old and weighed 345 pounds, topping his weight in Munich by 20 pounds. Alexeyev loved food (he was seen in Munich in 1972 eating a breakfast that included twenty-six eggs and a steak), but his increasing weight and lack of conditioning began to weaken him.

In October 1978 at the world championship in Gettysburg, Pennsylvania, Alexeyev looked fat and out of shape at 352 pounds. While dining on a platter of chicken before the competition, he told a journalist, "A great sportsman dies twice, and the first death is the more painful."[130] Alexeyev meant that an athlete's competitive life ends well before he dies. It was a prophecy he soon fulfilled.

Moscow was the last Olympics Alexeyev would compete in, but he went on to become head coach in the 1992 Olympics in Barcelona.

When Alexeyev tried his first lift of the meet, a tendon popped somewhere deep in his massive right hip and he had to withdraw, which meant an end to his string of eight world titles. The winner was Jurgen Heuser of East Germany, who had finished second to Alexeyev in the European championships.

Alexeyev's physical decline led to a swift descent from greatness. In the two years leading up to the 1980 Olympics in Moscow, Alexeyev was a man of mystery, training alone, if he was training at all, at home in Shakhty. He did not show up for the 1979 world championships in Greece and did not qualify for the 1980 Games until a few days before they began, when he easily lifted the qualifying weight. He was hugely fat, weighing 379 pounds, but slimmed down to 357 pounds for the competition.

When Alexeyev strode onto the lifting platform for the super-heavyweight event, he was greeted by Russian shouts of "My s toboi!" (We're with you!). But after failing to snatch 397 pounds on three attempts and almost falling while trying to get the weight up to his chest, Soviet fans turned against him. He left the platform to boos and loud, insulting whistles.

Although the career of the greatest weight lifter in Olympic history was over, Alexeyev was not ready to admit he had "died" for the first time. "I am an old and a very strong horse. You will see me again,"[131] he told reporters.

Olympic Coach

But Moscow was his last weight-lifting competition. Old, fat, and out of shape, Alexeyev retired and became a weight-lifting coach, continuing through the 1992 Olympics in Barcelona, Spain, when he was head coach. He then retired from the sport completely.

All Alexeyev's many records have been broken except for two, his Olympic marks for the press, no longer part of the competition, and total weight, which was for three lifts, not the two used today, which he set in 1972. Alexeyev, naturally, still retains his gold medals, as well as the reputation of the greatest weight lifter of all time.

Alexeyev once told a reporter, "Do not forget one thing. I am original. I am unique."[132]

And so he is.

CHAPTER 8

Eric Heiden: More than Just an Olympic Champion

Holding a corner of the Olympic flag in one strong hand, Eric Heiden softly intoned the athlete's oath in the opening ceremony of the 1980 Winter Games in Lake Placid, New York, promising to compete "in the true spirit of sportsmanship, for the glory of sport and the honor of our teams."[133]

Perhaps no athlete who recited that oath ever fulfilled more completely the ideals Pierre de Coubertin envisioned when he wrote those words. The speed skater won five gold medals at distances ranging from 500 meters to 10,000 meters, a feat comparable to winning every running event from the 100-meter dash to the marathon, while showing respect for his competitors, true love for his sport, and a refreshing absence of the egotism and arrogance of some Olympic champions.

Clad in his skintight gold racing suit, his impossibly huge thighs pumping like pistons as he zoomed over the ice, Heiden was a comic book superhero come to life, a golden blur racing his way into the history books. The shy, grinning skater from Madison, Wisconsin, left Lake Placid a sports superstar with the potential to extract more money from his gold medals than any athlete in history.

What Heiden did next astonished the world as much as his dominating performance. Although he accepted a few endorsement deals, Heiden turned down scores of other moneymaking opportunities. He said he didn't need all that money, that he preferred privacy to fame, that he wanted to get on with the *important* part of his life, which was to become an orthopedic surgeon like his father.

Unlike many Olympic champions who become intoxicated by fame, Heiden surrendered the easy life of a sports celebrity for the rigors of medical school and the long hours of a doctor. Former *Washington Post* reporter Sally Jenkins believes Heiden should be revered as much for his post-Olympic accomplishments as for his gold medals:

> What you do at twenty-one should not be the pinnacle of your entire life. And congratulations to him for building a life apart from his achievements. So many athletes live on it and dine out on it for the rest of their lives, and really are half people. Not Eric, he's a whole human being.[134]

The Athletic Heidens

Heiden was born June 14, 1958, into a Madison family that seemed destined to raise an Olympic champion. His grandfather, Art Thomsen, a former University of Wisconsin (UW) hockey coach, put Eric on skates when he was two years old; his mother, Nancy, was a fine skater, tennis player, swimmer, and cyclist; his father, Jack, a cocaptain of the UW fencing team in the 1950s, was a skier, skater, and in the 1970s a national champion in bicycle races for older riders.

Beth Heiden was born thirteen months later. Although a foot shorter and eighty pounds lighter than her big brother in 1980,

Eric Heiden won five gold medals at distances ranging from 500 meters to 10,000 meters.

when she would win an Olympic bronze speed skating medal, Beth helped make Eric work harder. They once talked of the sibling rivalry that made them compete in everything:

> Beth: We were doing chin-ups and both of us were convinced we were going to beat the other one.
>
> Eric: We got into a contest. You do one pull-up, I'll do one pull-up, you do two, I'll do two pull-ups.

On the advice of their parents, Eric and his sister, Beth, chose to concentrate on one sport—speed skating.

Beth: This kept going on. I did eight, he did eight. I did nine, he did nine. And then my dad came home.

Eric: He said, "You guys better cool it because you guys aren't going to stop until you get hurt."

Beth: Because neither one of us was going to give up.[135]

A few years after Eric began skating, he was whizzing over the wind-chilled, frozen lakes near Wisconsin's state capital, scoring goals in hockey and winning speed skating races. In the warmer months Eric played soccer and ran cross-country, Beth competed in track (she set a national record for the mile), and both Heidens raced bicycles. They even took up figure skating, although the two usually spent more time racing against each other.

Speed Skating Wins Out

When Eric was fourteen and Beth thirteen, their parents felt it was time for them to concentrate on one sport. It was a difficult decision, but Eric and Beth chose speed skating. In one of those quirks of fate that often determine destiny, they soon met someone who could guide them to greatness.

In 1972 Dianne Holum began attending UW on a scholarship. The Northbrook, Illinois, speed skater, who had won four Olympic medals including gold and silver in 1972 in Sapporo, Japan, began coaching the Madison Skating Club. Holum had to teach the Heidens a new style of speed skating as they made the switch from short-track (also called pack) to long-track racing, the style used in the Olympics.

In pack racing, which did not become an Olympic sport until 1992, skaters race in a group. There is a lot of bumping and shoving, and the winners are the first ones to cross the finish line. In long-track speed skating, which is contested on a 400-meter oval, skaters compete in pairs, and overall times for all skaters determine who wins.

Luckily for the Heidens, the nation's only Olympic-sized rink was located just seventy-five miles east in West Allis, a Milwaukee suburb that was the headquarters for U.S. speed skaters.

Becoming World Champions

Eric and Beth traveled almost daily during the winter to the outdoor rink at Wisconsin State Fair Park, which had a refrigeration system that could maintain ice even on warmer days. With Holum's help and Eric's propensity for long, grueling workouts, the teenager improved enough by 1975 to become a member of the U.S. Junior World Speedskating Team. Trips to Norway and the Netherlands became a treat for Eric:

> There is nothing like going to Europe and skating against the best in the world. Skating is a lot different in [Europe]. There, you're racing before twenty-five-thousand people. Here [in the United States] it's maybe a couple of dozen. Skating in Europe is like football here. I'd like to do what I can to make skating more popular in this country.[136]

Although Charles Jewtraw captured gold in 1924 in the 500-meter race in the first Winter Olympics, speed skating has always been a minor sport in America, drawing major attention only during Olympic years. In 1976 Eric and Beth qualified for their first Olympics, but neither was good enough to win in Innsbruck, Austria. Seventeen-year-old Eric finished seventh at 1,500 meters and nineteenth in the 5,000 meters, while Beth placed eleventh in the 3,000-meter race. It had been a promising Olympic debut, but what Eric did the next year shocked the speed skating world.

An Important Victory

Heiden simply became the most dominant skater in history by winning the World Junior Speedskating Championship (for younger skaters), the World Allround Speedskating Championship, and World Sprint Championship. Heiden was the first American to win a world title since 1891 and first skater from any country to capture all three world titles in the same year. He won the Allround title by beating the defending champion in the final race of 10,000 meters. Heiden knew right away how important his victory was:

> We're in Heerenveen [the Netherlands], which is like the Mecca of skating. I crossed that finish line and here I'd beat the Dutch champion, and yet the crowd is going crazy. They were giving me as much applause and admiration as they would any of their skaters. I'll tell you, that was like my coming out, I'd finally made it as a speed-skater.[137]

Although he had been short and slight as a young boy, Heiden by 1980 was 6 feet 1 inch tall and weighed a rock-solid 185 pounds, with a 32-inch waist and massive 29-inch thighs that gave him unequaled power. Heiden's technique was excellent, but it was his sheer, raw strength that made him unbeatable.

Dan Jansen of West Allis, who after bitter disappointments in two Olympics finally captured gold in the 1,000 meters in 1994, said the key to Heiden's success was his ability to work harder than anyone else. "Eric was such a freak of nature," says Jansen. "The guy could train like nobody else could train. He was so strong and he could handle any workload given to him."[138]

Heiden's workouts were killers and they did not stop in summer, when he would run 10 miles, cycle 100 miles, lift weights, and do a series of exhausting exercises to increase his strength and aerobic conditioning. Heiden also used an invention developed by a Soviet coach: special skates that had three narrow wheels in a line down the center of the skate, the forerunner of today's in-line skates.

During the winter Heiden would skate lap after punishing lap, working on his technique to start quickly and make turns at top speed. "I guess I'm kind of weird," he once said, "but I enjoy being tired."[139]

His tremendous work ethic helped Heiden win a succession of world titles in the three years leading up to the next Olympics. The last came in early February 1980, a few weeks before the Lake Placid Winter Games, when he won three of four races in West Allis to capture his fourth straight World Sprint Championship. Although Heiden suffered a rare defeat, losing a 500-meter race to teammate Tom Plant of West Allis, the news media were predicting that Heiden would win an unbelievable five gold medals. Instead of resenting the pressure, Heiden fed off the media's golden expectations:

> The nice thing is now you have a psychological edge on the other skaters. I'm looking forward to the Olympics now. It's probably within reach [five golds]. But it's going to be hard. There are a lot of good skaters. You have to think about the different races and different strategies for each race. And you never get a chance to relax [in ten days of competition].[140]

Olympic Perfection

Speed skaters wear "racing skins," one-piece, skin-tight suits made of stretch fabric that cuts wind resistance. In acknowledgment of Heiden's prowess, the 1980 U.S. Olympic team chose the color gold for its skins.

His shaggy, nearly shoulder-length brown hair tucked beneath his racing suit, Heiden moved confidently to the starting line of his

Running 10 miles, cycling 100 miles, and lifting weights were part of Heiden's tremendous work ethic that helped him win world titles.

first race, on February 15: the 500-meter event. By the luck of the prerace draw, when competitors' names are picked at random, Heiden was paired with Evgeni Kulikov of the Soviet Union, the 500-meter world record holder.

The two athletes toed the starting line, leaning forward while balancing on the tip of one skate. The gun sounded and they exploded off the line in short, choppy strides that dug into the ice as they built speed before settling into the longer, silky-smooth yet powerful strokes that carried them at top speed around the outdoor racing oval. The red-suited Kulikov had a narrow lead after 100 meters. But when he slipped in the first turn, Heiden pulled ahead and won in an Olympic record 38.03 seconds, just 0.34 second ahead of the Russian, who won silver.

The next day in the 5,000 meters, Heiden realized early in his race that he was 4 seconds behind the time already skated by Tom Eric Oxholm of Norway. So did his mother, who was frantic. "Oh, we've lost it," Nancy Heiden wailed when she saw his early lap times. "I know we've lost it. He's on too slow a time. He'll never make it up. We've lost it."[141]

Mom was wrong. Her son simply skated harder, pulling even with Oxholm's time by the 3,800-meter mark and finishing in 7:02.29 to shatter the Olympic record by 20 seconds. Heiden could not yet claim the gold, however, because world record holder Kai Arne Stenshjemmet of Norway had not skated. The Heiden family waited nervously for the Norwegian to take his turn, but he finished almost a full second behind Heiden.

Three days later Heiden won the 1,000-meter race in 1:15.18, another Olympic record, and two days later the 1,500 meters, which was nearly a disaster. Heiden slipped in the middle of the race and almost fell, but righted himself by shoving his hand against the ice. A slip usually costs a skater victory in lost time, but Heiden won again with an Olympic record 1:55.44.

After his fourth gold medal performance, Heiden told reporters he would rather be back at the Olympic Village with other athletes watching a movie than answering questions. The media blitz upset Heiden: not because he couldn't handle it, but because it was getting to be a burden even to his parents. "The Great Whoopee," Heiden derisively termed the overwhelming news coverage. "It's kind of a drag."[142]

The night before his final race, Heiden was a spectator for the U.S. ice hockey team's amazing 4–3 victory over the favored Soviet Union team, a win that propelled America into the gold medal game, which it won 4–2 over Finland for only its second gold medal in that sport in twenty years. At the hockey arena to cheer on childhood friends Mark Johnson and Bobby Suter, with whom he once played hockey, Heiden seemed more excited over their victory than any of his own.

Heiden stayed up so late celebrating the hockey team's victory that he almost missed his final race. Holum said Heiden overslept the next morning and she had to pound on his door to wake him up at 7:40 A.M., more than an hour later than he should have gotten up:

> We were waiting in the car to go to the rink, and he just wasn't there. I went back and went into his room, and he was still asleep. I had no idea he was out that night. I just woke him up, "Eric, you've got to be at the rink for warm-ups" [Holum said in a frantic voice]. So he quickly just threw everything together, ran into the cafeteria, grabbed bread, that's all he did was grab a bunch of bread and start shoving it into his mouth, and got ready for his race.[143]

At just over 6 miles and with 48 turns, the 10,000-meter race is a body-numbing test of endurance, and Heiden was already tired from four other races. His challenge became all the more difficult when Oxholm, skating ahead of him, posted a time of 14:36.60, just 1.5 seconds off the world record and almost 15 seconds faster than the Olympic record. But once again, America's golden boy was able to dig down deep into his seemingly inexhaustible inner reserves of physical and mental strength.

Heiden with the five gold medals he won in a clean sweep of all the men's speedskating events at the 1980 Olympics.

Skating with Viktor Leskin of the Soviet Union, Heiden quickly pulled ahead in the long, slow, rhythmic strides skaters use in longer races. Heiden now had only one foe, the clock, and once again he was victorious, chopping an incredible 6 seconds off the world record with a time of 14:28.13.

Heiden had become the first athlete to win five individual gold medals in a single Olympics. But when reporters asked if he knew of any greater Olympic accomplishment, Heiden modestly replied, "Sure, the United States hockey team has me beat."[144]

Handling Olympic Fame

The Olympics had exhausted Heiden physically. Worse, he had been sickened by the "Great Whoopee" and hated the lack of privacy that went with his newfound fame. The result was that he decided to quit speed skating, even though he could have continued to compete and, under new Olympic rules, make significant amounts of money even as an amateur. "Maybe if things had stayed the way they were and I could still be obscure in an obscure sport, I might want to keep skating," Heiden said. "I really liked it best when I was a nobody."[145]

Heiden for a brief time was the most marketable athlete on the planet. But there would be no poster with gold medals dangling around his neck, no movie roles, no series of well-paid public appearances. Art Kaminsky, a lawyer the Heiden family hired before the Olympics to help them cope with demands of the media and their son's fame, helped choose a few endorsements the family considered tasteful.

Becoming a "Productive Person"

It was now time for Heiden to get on with what he believed was the most important part of his life. Although Heiden still dabbled in athletic competition for several years by racing bicycles, even winning the U.S. Professional Championship in 1985, he began attending Stanford as a premed student. "Ever since I was a little kid, I wanted to be a doctor. But I had to put it on the back burner. You can only use that athletic talent when you're young,"[146] he said.

Heiden fulfilled his dream of following in his father's footsteps as an orthopedic surgeon, graduating in May 1991 from Stanford Medical School, and at age thirty-three beginning an internship in orthopedic surgery in Sacramento, California. In 1999 Heiden, who was practicing in Sacramento and married to Karen Drews,

Heiden fulfilled his dreams of becoming an orthopedic surgeon when he graduated from Stanford Medical School in 1991.

also an orthopedic surgeon, could say with pride: "Now I'm giving back to society, doing something important. I'm now what I consider a productive person in our society."[147]

Olympic Memories

Unlike many Olympic champions, Eric Heiden for the most part has made a break with the celebrity of his past, distancing himself from his past glory. In a magazine article in November 1998, Heiden admitted he had trouble keeping track of his five gold medals. Although he knew that four were at his parents' home in Madison, he had recently had trouble locating the fifth, which turned up on a closet floor buried under some clothes. "I guess I had thrown it in there awhile ago and forgotten about it," he says. "The 1980 Games seem like a lifetime ago."[148]

But Heiden's love of the Olympics has not waned, which is why he has been a television commentator at four Winter Games. "It's a blast to go back there. I get to relax and enjoy the atmosphere of the Olympics," Heiden said before the 1994 Games in Lillehammer, Norway. "The best thing is the credential that lets me go anywhere. I can do what I want, watch all the events I want to."[149]

The Greatness of the Games

From Coroebus, who in 776 B.C. won a footrace to become history's first recorded champion, to Carl Lewis, who in the centennial Summer Games in 1996 in Atlanta, Georgia, captured his ninth gold medal by winning the long jump, the Olympics have been a catalyst for athletic greatness.

Whether the athletes reshaped the boundaries of their sports in one stunning Olympics, as did Eric Heiden and Mark Spitz, or dominated through several competitions like Paavo Nurmi and Vasily Alexeyev, it is their performances that have made this quadrennial rite of sports so magnificent.

The seven athletes profiled here are only a small, representative sample of the champions who have graced the Olympics. Before Spitz there was Duke Paoa Kahanamoku, a member of Hawaiian royalty who won two gold medals in swimming in the 1920s and later introduced surfing to the world. And before the giant Alexeyev there was American weight lifter Tamio "Tommy" Kono, who from 1952 through 1960 won two gold medals and one silver.

Jim Thorpe was succeeded by America's Bob Mathias and England's Daley Thompson, who both won two consecutive decathlons, and Lewis in 1984 duplicated Owens's remarkable 1936 performance by winning the same four events.

If Olympic champions are judged by their gold medals, a little-known athlete from the Olympics' early days must be considered as the greatest Olympian: Ray Clarence Ewry, alias "the Rubber Man" and "Human Frog." The Lafayette, Indiana, native in 1900 won the standing high jump, standing long jump, and standing triple jump, events that were discontinued after 1912. Ewry from 1900 to 1908 won ten gold medals, more than any other athlete. Two of his golds, however, came in an unofficial 1906 Games held in Greece. But even eight was a remarkable achievement for an athlete who as a child had been confined to a wheelchair for several years with polio.

If Ewry is credited with only eight gold medals, he finishes second to three athletes who have won nine—Nurmi, Spitz, and Lewis. But many qualified observers believe Eric Heiden's performance in winning five individual gold medals was the finest in Olympic history. Among these expert commentators is award-winning filmmaker Bud Greenspan, who has chronicled the Games for more than four decades:

> Though Mark Spitz won seven gold medals in seven swimming events at the 1972 Munich games, Heiden's performance is considered greater. Heiden won all his races in individual events, while Spitz's momentous feat was attained in four individual events and as part of three relay teams.[150]

Olympic Mythology

The glory of such wonderful individual accomplishments has become secondary at times to the philosophical message promoted by officials who organize and run the Olympics. Starting with de Coubertin, Olympic officials have always tried to endow the games with semi-religious status.

In his memoirs, de Coubertin wrote that "sport is a religion with church, dogma, ritual" and in a radio address August 4, 1935, claimed the Olympics were "religious sentiment transformed and enlarged by the internationalism and democracy that distinguish the modern age." Nearly three decades later Avery Brundage, the most powerful and dictatorial of International Olympic Committee (IOC) presidents, said that "Olympism," the term de Coubertin coined for the morality underlying the Olympics, is "a religion with universal appeal which incorporates all the basic values of other religions, a modern, exciting, virile, dynamic religion."[151]

Yet historian William Oscar Johnson believes those sentiments sometimes hurt the Olympics:

> It is their mythology which makes [them] seem such a force for cynicism and hypocrisy. It is the attempt to clothe the games in grand ideals they could never realize which makes them seem so fallible, so undermined and so corrupted by man's meanest motives.[152]

Ray Clarence Ewry (second row, third from left) won a total of ten gold medals, more than any other athlete.

Johnson is critical of the excessive nationalism that has tarnished the Olympics, their increasing commercialism in the twentieth century, and problems in defining the "amateur" athlete. And although Johnson wrote the phrase long before the 1999 scandal over the 2002 Winter Olympics in Salt Lake City, Utah, his claim that Olympics ideals have often been "corrupted by man's meanest motives" is an apt commentary on the behavior of some IOC members.

Although the Salt Lake City scandal tainted the Olympics heading into the new millennium, the performances of athletes in the 2000 Summer Games in Sydney, Australia, and in the 2002 Winter Games will surely help to heal any damage that has been done. Such individual moments of athletic greatness are, after all, the very essence of the Olympic Games.

NOTES

Introduction: The Olympic Champion: Swifter, Higher, Stronger

1. Quoted in Lord Killanin and John Rodda, eds., *The Olympic Games: 80 Years of People, Events and Records*. New York: CollierBooks, 1976, p. 14.

2. Dave Anderson, *The Story of the Olympics*. New York: Beech Tree Paperback, 1996, p. 131.

3. Quoted in William Oscar Johnson Jr., *The Olympics: A History of the Games*, 2nd printing. New York: Time Inc., 1993, p. 9.

Chapter 1: Evolution of the Olympic Games

4. Quoted in Johnson, *The Olympics*, p. 13.

5. Quoted in Dick Schaap, *An Illustrated History of the Olympics*, 3rd ed. New York: Knopf, 1975, p. 38.

6. Quoted in Johnson, *The Olympics*, p. 13.

7. Quoted in Allen Guttmann, *The Olympics: A History of the Modern Games*. Chicago: University of Illinois Press, 1992, p. 11.

8. Quoted in Ron Thomas and Joe Herran, *The Grolier Student Encyclopedia of the Olympic Games*. Danbury, CT: Grolier Educational, 1996, p. 70.

9. Schaap, *An Illustrated History of the Olympics*, p. vii.

10. Quoted in John A. Lucas, *Future of the Olympic Games*. Champaign, IL: Human Kinetics Books, 1992, p. 4.

11. Killanin and Rodda, eds., *The Olympic Games*, p. 59.

12. Quoted in Guttmann, *The Olympics*, p. 97.

13. Quoted in Jeffrey O. Segrave and Donald Chu, eds., *The Olympic Games in Transition*. Champaign, IL: Human Kinetics Books, 1988, p. 255.

14. Quoted in David Wallechinsky, *The Complete Book of the Olympics: 1992 Edition*. Boston: Little, Brown, 1992, p. xxiv.

15. Quoted in William O. Johnson Jr., *All That Glitters Is Not Gold: The Olympic Game*. New York: G. P. Putnam's Sons, 1972, p. 20.

16. Quoted in Judith Pinkerton Josephson, *Jesse Owens: Track and Field Legend*. Springfield, NJ: Enslow Publishers, 1997, p. 84.

17. Lucas, *Future of the Olympic Games,* p. 15.

18. Larry Siddons, *The Olympics at 100: A Celebration in Pictures.* New York: Macmillan USA, 1995, p. 104.

19. Siddons, *The Olympics at 100,* p. 165.

20. Johnson, *All That Glitters Is Not Gold,* p. 39.

Chapter 2: Jim Thorpe: The Most Tragic Olympic Champion

21. Quoted in Don Nardo, *The Importance of Jim Thorpe.* San Diego: Lucent Books, 1994, p. 70.

22. Quoted in Robert W. Wheeler, *Jim Thorpe: World's Greatest Athlete.* Norman: University of Oklahoma Press, 1975, p. 9.

23. Quoted in Wheeler, *Jim Thorpe,* p. 36.

24. Quoted in Associated Press and Grolier, *Pursuit of Excellence: The Olympic Story.* Danbury, CT: Grolier Enterprises, 1983, p. 69.

25. Quoted in John Devaney, *Great Olympic Champions.* New York: G. P. Putnam's Sons, 1967, p. 32.

26. Quoted in Associated Press and Grolier, *Pursuit of Excellence,* p. 69.

27. Quoted in Schaap, *An Illustrated History of the Olympics,* p. 126.

28. Quoted in Devaney, *Great Olympic Champions,* p. 32.

29. Quoted in Wheeler, *Jim Thorpe,* p. 100.

30. Quoted in Associated Press and Grolier, *Pursuit of Excellence,* p. 68.

31. Quoted in Wallechinsky, *The Complete Book of the Olympics,* p. 125.

32. Quoted in Nardo, *Jim Thorpe,* p. 49.

33. Quoted in Wallechinsky, *The Complete Book of the Olympics,* p. 125.

34. Quoted in Nardo, *Jim Thorpe,* p. 54.

35. Quoted in Devaney, *Great Olympic Champions,* p. 40.

36. Quoted in Sam Levy, "Jim Thorpe Visits Town and Recalls Days on Brewers," *Milwaukee Journal,* May 6, 1951.

37. Quoted in Myron Cope, *The Game That Was: The Early Days of Pro Football.* New York: World Publishing Company, 1970, p. 28.

38. Quoted in Johnson, *All That Glitters Is Not Gold,* p. 135.

39. Quoted in Associated Press and Grolier, *Pursuit of Excellence,* p. 70.

Chapter 3: Paavo Nurmi: Winning with "Sisu"

40. K. P. Silberg, *The Athletic Finn.* Hancock, MI: Suomi Publishing Company, 1927, pp. 84–85.

41. Quoted in Johnson, *The Olympics,* p. 72.

42. Devaney, *Great Olympic Champions,* p. 42.

43. Quoted in Killanin and Rodda, eds., *The Olympic Games,* p. 48.

44. Quoted in Silberg, *The Athletic Finn,* p. 107.

45. Quoted in Devaney, *Great Olympic Champions,* p. 51.

46. Quoted in Silberg, *The Athletic Finn,* pp. 141–42.

47. Quoted in Silberg, *The Athletic Finn,* pp. 123–24.

48. Silberg, *The Athletic Finn,* pp. 130–31.

49. Quoted in Devaney, *Great Olympic Champions,* p. 53.

50. Johnson, *All That Glitters Is Not Gold,* p. 142.

51. Quoted in Associated Press and Grolier, *Pursuit of Excellence,* p. 45.

Chapter 4: Jesse Owens: Hero of the "Nazi Olympics"

52. Quoted in Associated Press and Grolier, *Pursuit of Excellence,* p. 150.

53. Quoted in Richard D. Mandell, *The Nazi Olympics.* New York: Macmillan, 1971, p. 236.

54. Quoted in Joseph J. Vecchione, ed., *The New York Times Book of Sports Legends.* New York: Times Books, 1991, p. 235.

55. Quoted in Josephson, *Jesse Owens,* p. 16.

56. Quoted in Johnson, *All That Glitters Is Not Gold,* p. 50.

57. Quoted in Josephson, *Jesse Owens,* p. 20.

58. Quoted in Devaney, *Great Olympic Champions,* p. 81.

59. Quoted in Josephson, *Jesse Owens,* p. 18.

60. Quoted in Josephson, *Jesse Owens,* p. 24.

61. Quoted in Vecchione, *The New York Times Book of Sports Legends,* p. 235.

62. Quoted in Guttmann, *The Olympics,* p. 58.

63. Quoted in Johnson, *All That Glitters Is Not Gold,* p. 176.

64. Quoted in Larry Siddons, *The Olympics at 100*, p. 48.

65. Quoted in Guttmann, *The Olympics*, p. 68.

66. Quoted in Josephson, *Jesse Owens*, p. 10.

67. Quoted in Associated Press and Grolier, *Pursuit of Excellence*, p. 12.

68. Quoted in Wallechinsky, *The Complete Book of the Olympics*, p. 99.

69. Quoted in Bud Greenspan, *100 Greatest Moments in Olympic History*. Los Angeles: General Publishing Group, 1995, p. 19.

70. Quoted in Greenspan, *100 Greatest Moments in Olympic History*, p. 19.

71. Quoted in Devaney, *Great Olympic Champions*, p. 84.

72. Quoted in Josephson, *Jesse Owens*, p. 69.

73. Quoted in Johnson, *All That Glitters Is Not Gold*, p. 179.

74. Quoted in Josephson, *Jesse Owens*, p. 69.

75. Quoted in Johnson, *The Olympics*, p. 71.

76. Quoted in Johnson, *The Olympics*, p. 71.

77. Quoted in Johnson, *The Olympics*, p. 71.

78. Johnson, *All That Glitters Is Not Gold*, p. 44.

Chapter 5: Jean-Claude Killy: Racing to Glory

79. Quoted in Associated Press and Grolier, *Pursuit of Excellence*, p. 276.

80. Quoted in Associated Press and Grolier, *Pursuit of Excellence*, p. 276.

81. Quoted in Phil Hersh, "To Olympus and Back," *Sports Illustrated*, November 18, 1991, Special Advertising Section.

82. Jean-Claude Killy and Al Greenberg, *Comeback*. New York: Macmillan, 1974, p. 18.

83. Quoted in Associated Press and Grolier, *Pursuit of Excellence*, p. 276.

84. Quoted in Killy and Greenberg, *Comeback*, p. 45.

85. Quoted in Killy and Greenberg, *Comeback*, p. 45.

86. Quoted in John Skow, "In Search of Killy," *Skiing*, January 1992.

87. Quoted in Johnson, *The Olympics*, p. 144.

88. Killy and Greenberg, *Comeback*, p. 21.

89. Killy and Greenberg, *Comeback*, p. 31.

90. Killy and Greenberg, *Comeback*, p. 24.

91. Killy and Greenberg, *Comeback*, p. 32.

92. Quoted in Martin Connors, Diane L. Dupuis, and Brad Morgan, *The Olympics Factbook: A Spectator's Guide to the Winter and Summer Games.* Detroit: Visible Ink Press, 1992, p. 131.

93. Quoted in Associated Press and Grolier, *Pursuit of Excellence,* p. 277.

94. Quoted in Associated Press and Grolier, *Pursuit of Excellence,* p. 277.

95. Killy and Greenberg, *Comeback*, p. 36.

96. Quoted in Skow, "In Search of Killy."

97. Quoted in Hersh, "To Olympus and Back."

98. Quoted in Skow, "In Search of Killy."

Chapter 6: Mark Spitz: Olympic Glory Dimmed by Olympic Tragedy

99. Quoted in Associated Press and Grolier, *Pursuit of Excellence,* p. 303.

100. Quoted in Associated Press and Grolier, *Pursuit of Excellence,* p. 303.

101. Mark Spitz and Alan LeMond, *The Mark Spitz Complete Book of Swimming.* New York: Thomas Y. Crowell, 1976, p. 8.

102. Quoted in Associated Press and Grolier, *Pursuit of Excellence,* p. 304.

103. Spitz and LeMond, *The Mark Spitz Complete Book of Swimming,* p. 4.

104. Spitz and LeMond, *The Mark Spitz Complete Book of Swimming,* p. 3.

105. Quoted in Associated Press and Grolier, *Pursuit of Excellence,* p. 304.

106. Quoted in Kenny Moore, "Bionic Man: At 39, Mark Spitz, Winner of Seven Golds at the 1972 Games, Is Trying What No Mere Mortal Would—An Olympic Comeback." *Sports Illustrated,* November 23, 1989.

107. Quoted in Jerry Kirshenbaum, "Mark of Excellence," *Sports Illustrated*, August 14, 1972.

108. Quoted in Associated Press and Grolier, *Pursuit of Excellence*, p. 304.

109. Quoted in Greenspan, *100 Greatest Moments in Olympic History*, p. 196.

110. Quoted in Greenspan, *100 Greatest Moments in Olympic History*, p. 196.

111. Jerry Kirshenbaum, "A Sanctuary Violated," *Sports Illustrated*, September 18, 1972.

112. Quoted in Killanin and Rodda, eds., *The Olympic Games*, p. 21.

113. Quoted in Kirshenbaum, "A Sanctuary Violated."

114. Quoted in Johnson, *The Olympics*, p. 147.

115. Quoted in Sam Allis, "Testing the Limits of Middle Age," *Time*, May 21, 1990.

116. Quoted in Allis, "Testing the Limits of Middle Age."

Chapter 7: Vasily Alexeyev: The Soviet Hercules

117. Yuri Brokhin, *The Big Red Machine: The Rise and Fall of Soviet Olympic Champions*. New York: Random House, 1978, p. 194.

118. Interview with the author, March 7, 1999.

119. Quoted in Brokhin, *The Big Red Machine*, p. 216.

120. Quoted in Brokhin, *The Big Red Machine*, p. 218.

121. Interview with the author, March 7, 1999.

122. Interview with the author, March 7, 1999.

123. Quoted in Johnson, *The Olympics*, p. 148.

124. Quoted in William O. Johnson, "The Best at Everything," *Sports Illustrated*, April 14, 1975.

125. Quoted in Johnson, "The Best at Everything."

126. Quoted in Johnson, "The Best at Everything."

127. Quoted in Anita Verschoth, "Now Maybe His Wife Will Listen," *Sports Illustrated*, August 9, 1976.

128. Brokhin, *The Big Red Machine*, p. 223.

129. Quoted in Verschoth, "Now Maybe His Wife Will Listen."

130. Quoted in Bruce Newman, "Russia Keeps Coming on Strong," *Sports Illustrated*, October 16, 1978.

131. Quoted in B. J. Phillips, "You Will See Me Again . . . ," *Time*, August 11, 1980.

132. Quoted in Johnson, "The Best at Everything."

Chapter 8: Eric Heiden: More Than Just an Olympic Champion

133. Quoted in Thomas and Herran, *The Grolier Student Encyclopedia of the Olympic Games*, p. 70.

134. Quoted on ESPN, "Sports Century Top 50 Countdown: Eric Heiden," aired November 18, 1998, 30 minutes.

135. Quoted on ESPN, "Sports Century Top 50 Countdown: Eric Heiden."

136. Quoted in Mary Virginia Fox, *The Skating Heidens.* Hillside, NJ: Enslow Publishers, 1981, p. 38.

137. Quoted on ESPN, "Sports Century Top 50 Countdown: Eric Heiden."

138. Quoted on ESPN, "Sports Century Top 50 Countdown: Eric Heiden."

139. Quoted in Associated Press and Grolier, *Pursuit of Excellence,* p. 352.

140. Quoted in Michael V. Uschan, "Heiden Wins 'Good Tuneup,'" *United Press International*, February 11, 1980.

141. Quoted in E. M. Swift, "Look, Ma, Two Golds," *Sports Illustrated*, February 27, 1980.

142. Quoted in E. M. Swift, "The Big Whoopee," *Sports Illustrated*, March 3, 1980.

143. Quoted on ESPN, "Sports Century Top 50 Countdown: Eric Heiden."

144. Quoted in Nathan Aaseng, *Eric Heiden: Winner in Gold.* Minneapolis: Lerner Publications, 1980, p. 50.

145. Quoted in Wallechinsky, *The Complete Book of the Olympics,* p. 719.

146. Quoted in Johnson, *The Olympics,* p. 188.

147. Quoted on ESPN, "Sports Century Top 50 Countdown: Eric Heiden."

148. Quoted in L. Jon Wertheim, "Still Handy with Blades: Not That Long Ago Self-Effacing Surgeon Eric Heiden Was an Olympic Hero," *Sports Illustrated*, November 16, 1998.

149. Quoted in Michael V. Uschan, "Heiden's Back at Olympics, but Behind a Mike," Associated Press, January 31, 1994.

Epilogue: The Greatness of the Games

150. Greenspan, *100 Greatest Moments in Olympic History,* p. 55.

151. Quoted in Guttmann, *The Olympics,* p. 3.

152. Johnson, *The Olympics,* p. 292.

CHRONOLOGY

776 B.C.
Coroebus wins a footrace to become the first recorded Olympic champion.

A.D. 394
Roman emperor Theodosius bans the Olympics as a pagan festival dedicated to the Greek god Zeus.

1896
Three hundred eleven athletes from thirteen nations compete in Athens, Greece, in the first modern Olympics.

1900
In Paris, France, cricket and croquet make their only appearance as Olympic sports.

1904
The first Olympics held in America takes place in St. Louis, Missouri; George Poage of the Milwaukee Athletic Club becomes the first African American to win a medal, taking third in the 400-meter hurdles.

1906
Greece holds an interim event in Athens. The only competition held outside the standard four-year cycle, it is not considered an official Olympics.

1912
Jim Thorpe wins the pentathlon and decathlon in Stockholm, Sweden.

1916
Cancellation of the Olympic Games due to World War I.

1920
The Olympic flag and Olympic oath for athletes are introduced in Antwerp, Belgium; Paavo Nurmi competes in his first Olympics and in three Summer Games wins nine gold medals and three silver.

1924
Two hundred ninety-three athletes from sixty-seven nations compete in the first Winter Games in Chamonix, France.

1928
In Amsterdam, Holland, an Olympic flame burns for the first time during the Summer Games.

1932
The Winter Games are held in Lake Placid, New York, and the Summer Games in Los Angeles, California.

1936

Jesse Owens wins four gold medals in Berlin, Germany, to shatter Adolf Hitler's theory of Aryan supremacy; for the first time the Olympic flame is lit in Greece and carried to the site of the Games by a relay of runners bearing torches.

1940 and 1944

Cancellation of two Olympic cycles due to World War II.

1948

The Olympics resume in London, England. Bob Mathias, a seventeen-year-old California high school student, wins the first of two consecutive gold medals in the decathlon.

1952

Richard Button wins his second gold medal in figure skating in Oslo, Norway.

1956

The first Olympic Games in the Southern Hemisphere are held in Melbourne, Australia; athletes for the first time march into the closing ceremony together instead of being separated by country.

1960

In Rome, Italy, Abebe Bikila, a private in the Ethiopian Imperial Bodyguard, runs the marathon on bare feet and breaks Czechoslovakian Emil Zatopek's Olympic record by almost 8 minutes.

1964

In Tokyo, Japan, Joe Frazier of the United States wins a gold medal in heavyweight boxing.

1968

Jean-Claude Killy sweeps the three Alpine skiing events in Grenoble, France; in the high altitude of Mexico City, Bob Beamon sets a world record for the long jump of 29 feet, 2 1/2 inches that will stand for three decades.

1972

Mark Spitz wins seven gold medals in swimming in Munich, Germany; the world is horrified by the slaying of eleven Israeli athletes taken hostage by a terrorist group.

1976

Vasily Alexeyev wins his second gold medal in weight lifting.

1980

Eric Heiden sweeps the gold in five speed skating races in Lake Placid, New York; the United States and 61 other nations boycott the Summer Games in Moscow, Russia, because the Soviet Union has invaded Afghanistan.

1984

In retaliation for the 1980 U.S. boycott, the Soviet Union and 13 of its allies send no athletes to the Summer Games in Los Angeles.

1988

In Seoul, Korea, American Greg Louganis becomes the first to repeat as a double gold medalist in both the springboard and platform diving events.

1992

In Barcelona, Spain, American Carl Lewis wins his seventh and eighth gold medals, including his third straight in the long jump.

1994

Because the International Olympic Committee decided to start alternating the Summer and Winter Games every two years, the Winter Games are held in Lillehammer, Norway, two years after the last Winter Olympics.

1996

In the Winter Games in Nagano, Japan, the U.S. luge team wins its first medals ever, silver and bronze by the doubles teams of Gordy Sheer–Chris Thorpe and Mark Grimmette–Brian Martin; in the centennial Summer Olympics in Atlanta, Georgia, Carl Lewis wins his fourth straight long jump and ninth gold medal.

FOR FURTHER READING

Dave Anderson, *The Story of the Olympics*. New York: Beech Tree Paperback, 1996. An easy-to-read, insightful history of American participation in the Olympics.

Stan Cohen, *The Games of '36: A Pictorial History of the 1936 Olympics in Germany*. Missoula, MT: Pictorial Histories Publishing Company, 1996. The drama of the 1936 Olympics is brought alive in a wonderful collection of pictures and accompanying text that explains the historical context in which the Games took place.

John Devaney, *Great Olympic Champions*. New York: G. P. Putnam's Sons, 1967. Well-written, short biographies of more than a dozen champions.

Mary Virginia Fox, *The Skating Heidens*. Hillside, NJ: Enslow Publishers, 1981. An excellent biography for younger readers of Eric Heiden and his sister, Beth.

William Heuman, *Famous American Athletes*. New York: Dodd, Mead, 1963. Short biographies of some of the greatest figures in American sports history, including Jim Thorpe and Jesse Owens.

William Oscar Johnson Jr., *The Olympics: A History of the Games*, 2nd printing. New York: Time Inc., 1993. A solid, well-documented history of the Olympics by a sportswriter who reported on many Olympics and has strong ideas on what is wrong and right with the Games.

Judith Pinkerton Josephson, *Jesse Owens: Track and Field Legend*. Springfield, NJ: Enslow Publishers, 1997. A biography rich in detail on the life of Jesse Owens.

Lord Killanin and John Rodda, eds., *The Olympic Games: 80 Years of People, Events and Records*. New York: CollierBooks, 1976. Killanin, a former president of the International Olympic Committee, and Rodda, a journalist, explain the history of the Olympics through writings of athletes and others who have participated in the Games.

Richard D. Mandell, *The Nazi Olympics*. New York: Macmillan, 1971. One of the best accounts available of the 1936 Olympics, providing an intriguing look into how Adolf Hitler used the Games to promote his nation and his racist philosophy.

Don Nardo, *The Importance of Jim Thorpe*. San Diego: Lucent Books, 1994. A well-written biography of one of America's greatest sports figures.

Dick Schaap, *An Illustrated History of the Olympics*, 3rd ed. New York: Knopf, 1975. This history by one of America's best sportswriters is lavishly illustrated with photographs that bring the past alive.

Larry Siddons, *The Olympics at 100: A Celebration in Pictures*. New York: Macmillan USA, 1995. A concise history written by a sports editor for Associated Press that features excellent pictures by AP photographers.

Ron Thomas and Joe Herran, *The Grolier Student Encyclopedia of the Olympic Games*. Danbury, CT: Grolier Educational, 1996. An excellent reference book for younger readers that explains the Olympics.

David Wallechinsky, *The Complete Book of the Olympics: 1992 Edition*. Boston: Little, Brown, 1992. A thorough history of the Summer and Winter Olympics through 1988; contains fascinating facts about medal winners and results from every event.

Works Consulted

Books

Nathan Aaseng, *Eric Heiden: Winner in Gold.* Minneapolis: Lerner Publications, 1980. A short biography with the basic facts of Heiden's life up to his Olympic triumphs, written for the younger reader.

Associated Press and Grolier, *Pursuit of Excellence: The Olympic Story.* Danbury, CT: Grolier Enterprises, 1983. A detailed look into Olympic history, including biographical material about major participants and how the Summer and Winter Games have evolved.

Yuri Brokhin, *The Big Red Machine: The Rise and Fall of Soviet Olympic Champions.* New York: Random House, 1978. Brokhin, a Russian journalist who immigrated to America, offers an in-depth look at how the former Soviet Union worked to mass produce Olympic champions.

Martin Connors, Diane L. Dupuis, and Brad Morgan, *The Olympics Factbook: A Spectator's Guide to the Winter and Summer Games.* Detroit: Visible Ink Press, 1992. One of the best sources for facts and figures on the Olympics, this book also contains details on the individual sports in the Summer and Winter Games and a basic history of the Olympics.

Myron Cope, *The Game That Was: The Early Days of Pro Football.* New York: World Publishing Company, 1970. An interesting history of how pro football began based on interviews with Hall of Fame players.

Bud Greenspan, *100 Greatest Moments in Olympic History.* Los Angeles: General Publishing Group, 1995. Greenspan, who has won international acclaim for films about the Olympics, writes movingly about the finest performances in Olympic history.

Allen Guttmann, *The Olympics: A History of the Modern Games.* Chicago: University of Illinois Press, 1992. A scholarly look at Olympic history that keys on the social and political forces that have shaped its evolution.

William O. Johnson Jr., *All That Glitters Is Not Gold: The Olympic Game.* New York: G. P. Putnam's Sons, 1972. A critical, sometimes negative look by a veteran sportswriter at how the Olympics have fared through the decades.

Jean-Claude Killy and Al Greenberg, *Comeback*. New York: Macmillan, 1974. An autobiography focusing on Killy's return to competition in 1972; also provides valuable insights about the skier's childhood and rise to Olympic glory.

David A. Klatell and Norman Marcus, *Sports for Sale: Television, Money, and the Fans*. New York: Oxford University Press, 1988. The authors trace the historical development of Olympic commercialism, especially as it relates to rights to televise the Games.

John A. Lucas, *Future of the Olympic Games*. Champaign, IL: Human Kinetics Books, 1992. Lucas, who has written extensively about the Olympics, provides an insider's knowledge about the Olympic bureaucracy. Lucas, however, often defends Olympic officials instead of considering issues objectively.

Jeffrey O. Segrave and Donald Chu, eds., *The Olympic Games in Transition*. Champaign, IL: Human Kinetics Books, 1988. Commentaries by historians, athletes, journalists, and scholars that shed light on many facets of Olympic history and key issues that have affected the Games.

K. P. Silberg, *The Athletic Finn*. Hancock, MI: Suomi Publishing Company, 1927. Written decades ago at the height of Paavo Nurmi's fame, this quaint book provides interesting insights into the impact of Nurmi and other Finnish runners on the world of sports.

Mark Spitz and Alan LeMond, *The Mark Spitz Complete Book of Swimming*. New York: Thomas Y. Crowell, 1976. In addition to explaining the basics of swimming, Spitz provides interesting autobiographical material on his competitive days.

Bill Toomey and Barry King, *The Olympic Challenge 1988*. Costa Mesa, CA: HDL Publishing, 1988. A fact-filled look at Olympic history and issues by Toomey, the 1968 decathlon champion, and King, a journalist.

Joseph J. Vecchione, ed., *The New York Times Book of Sports Legends*. New York: Times Books, 1991. Biographies by *New York Times* writers of some of the world's most famous sports figures, including several Olympic champions.

Robert W. Wheeler, *Jim Thorpe: World's Greatest Athlete*. Norman: University of Oklahoma Press, 1975. The most thoroughly researched biography written about Thorpe, it contains primary source quotes from Thorpe, family members, and people he met throughout his life.

Periodicals

Sam Allis, "Testing the Limits of Middle Age," *Time*, May 21, 1990.

Phil Hersh, "To Olympus and Back," *Sports Illustrated*, November 18, 1991, Special Advertising Section.

William O. Johnson, "The Best at Everything," *Sports Illustrated*, April 14, 1975.

Jerry Kirshenbaum, "Mark of Excellence," *Sports Illustrated*, August 14, 1972.

————, "A Sanctuary Violated," *Sports Illustrated*, September 18, 1972.

Kenny Moore, "Bionic Man: At 39, Mark Spitz, Winner of Seven Golds at the 1972 Games, Is Trying What No Mere Mortal Would—An Olympic Comeback," *Sports Illustrated*, November 23, 1989.

Bruce Newman, "Russia Keeps Coming on Strong," *Sports Illustrated*, October 16, 1978.

B. J. Phillips, "You Will See Me Again . . ." *Time*, August 11, 1980.

John Skow, "In Search of Killy," *Skiing*, January 1992.

E. M. Swift, "Look, Ma, Two Golds," *Sports Illustrated*, February 27, 1980.

————, "The Big Whoopee," *Sports Illustrated*, March 3, 1980.

Anita Verschoth, "Now Maybe His Wife Will Listen," *Sports Illustrated*, August 9, 1976.

L. Jon Wertheim, "Still Handy with Blades: Not That Long Ago Self-Effacing Surgeon Eric Heiden Was an Olympic Hero," *Sports Illustrated*, November 16, 1998.

Newspapers

Sam Levy, "Jim Thorpe Visits Town and Recalls Days on Brewers," *Milwaukee Journal*, May 6, 1951.

Michael V. Uschan, "Heiden's Back at Olympics, but Behind a Mike," Associated Press, January 31, 1994.

———, "Heiden Wins 'Good Tuneup,'" United Press International, February 11, 1980.

Video

ESPN, "Sports Century Top 50 Countdown: Eric Heiden," aired November 18, 1998, 30 minutes.

INDEX

Junior World Speedskating
   Team, 90
   Nurmi's visit to, 43

Val-d'Isére, France, 59

Wallechinsky, David, 19
Warner, Glenn, 26, 27, 29
weightlifting, types of, 78
Weiner, Suzy, 74
Weissmuller, Johnny, 74
West Point Academy, 31
Wieslander, Hugo, 31
Wilson, James, 40

Wing, John Ian, 16
Wisconsin State Fair Park, 89
Woelke, Hans, 52
women, 14
World Allround Speedskating
   Championship, 90
World Junior Speedskating
   Championship, 90
World Sprint Championship, 90
World War I, 17
World War II, 17

Zhabotinsky, Leonid, 78

PICTURE CREDITS

ABOUT THE AUTHOR

Michael V. Uschan has written eight books including a biography of golfer Tiger Woods and *A Basic Guide to Luge,* one of a series written for the U.S. Olympic Committee. Mr. Uschan began his career as a writer and editor with United Press International, a wire service that provides news reports to newspapers, radio, and television. Because journalism is sometimes called "history in a hurry," he considers writing history books a natural extension of the skills he developed as a journalist. The author covered many sporting events for United Press International and still writes sports stories for Associated Press. Mr. Uschan wrote many stories for United Press International about speed skater Eric Heiden and his quest for five gold medals. He and his wife, Barbara, live in Franklin, Wisconsin, a suburb of Milwaukee.